Simple Pleasures

Shirley Cole Barker

PublishAmerica
Baltimore

ISBN: 1-60703-045-4
PUBLISHED BY PUBLISHAMERICA, LLLP
www.publishamerica.com
Baltimore

Printed in the United States of America

I dedicate this book to my soul mate, James, and to our family.

To our children: Kyle, Kurt and Audrey

Our grandchildren: Scott, Candice, Gabrielle and Nathan

And our great-grandchildren: Caylin, Mason, Bryce and Dylan

May you read this book and remember the generations who came before you.

May you continue to protect the principles and traditions of the
Heritage left to you by your forefathers; they did not always come easy.

Acknowledgments

This book would not have been possible without some very special people in my life. I would like to acknowledge these people, many of whom are in Heaven today.

First, my grandmother, Mary Leola Cole, or "Ma," influenced my life greatly. Her loving spirit and Christian testimony were so very evident in her day-to-day walk.

Secondly, my parents, Evins and Ray Cole, gave me life, love and a Christian guideline to follow as a child and into my adult years.

To my siblings, Bonnie, Mearl and Barbara, thank you for putting up with your baby sister. Perhaps that was not always an easy thing to do. I love you.

My best friend, Sherry Brown Borgers, her mother and my second mother, Loretta Brown, helped me with many details of this book. Thank you for the memories.

Encouragers are so important. Thank you to those of you who read my story in the newspaper and encouraged me to put it into book form.

And finally, to my husband, James, I owe a great deal of gratitude. Thank you for sharing me with my computer for many, many days and evenings.

Contents

Introduction 9

The Steiner Years...

    1: Family History and History of Steiner . 13

    2: My Birth and Early Life 24

    3: Surviving the Lean Years 34

    4: Steiner Store 51

    5: My Home... 66

    6: My Playground and Playmates............ 81

    7: School Days 95

    8: Fun and Entertainment 105

    9: Remember the Sabbath Day 121

The Meridian Years...

    10: Lake Whitney—The End of an Era

    Meridian—A New Beginning 141

Reflections... 163

Introduction

Once upon a time long, long ago, a little girl named Shirley Glenda Cole was born. That little girl lived at Steiner, Texas, for the first nine years of her life. She loved Steiner, but shortly after her ninth birthday, she moved with her family to Meridian, Texas. Both Steiner and Meridian left their mark on the little girl. So much so that she wrote a story about her life at Steiner and about the first few years after she moved to Meridian.

The little girl would love to say she grew up to be a fairy princess, but that would not be true. In reality, the little girl grew up to be an ordinary person with an ordinary story to tell. And now the grown-up little girl wants to tell her story while she still remembers how she felt when she was that little girl growing up at Steiner and Meridian.

I hope the story about the little girl will be as enjoyable for you to read as it was for me to write.

The Steiner Years…

- 1 -

Family History and History of Steiner

Memories of my early life have been tucked away in my head for almost sixty years now. It is time for me to go back and celebrate those years the best way I know how—by remembering all the wonderful times I had living in Steiner, Texas. I close my eyes and the years begin to move in reverse, slowly ticking backward, to a time of childhood innocence. My story is not one that can be summed up in two or three pages. As you read, remember that an adult is telling the story; yet it is seen through the eyes of a child no more than nine years of age.

My father's parents, James William and Mary Leola (Wiggins) Cole, were married January 21, 1896 in Alabama. In 1901, they came to Texas in a covered wagon along with James William's parents,

John Randolph and Mariah Elizabeth (Cosper) Cole, and other family members. Initially, they settled in the Meridian area because Mariah already had family members living in Meridian at that time. James William and Mary Leola Cole later moved to Dyersville, a small community near Steiner. They had four children: Arnold David, Lois Alvin, Evins Mearl and Lula Eunita. My dad, Evins, was born December 10, 1908.

My mother's parents, James Mattison and Laura (Pinnell) Allen, were married September 9, 1906 and lived in the Spring Creek community near Meridian. They had four children: Florence Ray, Velma Elizabeth, Elmer Odell and Leonard Owen. Florence Ray, my mother, was born June 8, 1907. In January 1919, when my mother was not yet twelve years old, her mother, Laura Allen, died. At that time my mother went to live with her uncle, Otho Pinnell, and his wife in the Dyersville community.

Since Dyersville was a small community, my parents, Evins and Ray Cole, grew up knowing each other. After a brief courtship they were married on December 24, 1929 at Kopperl, Texas. Brother Billy Greer, pastor of Steiner Baptist Church, performed the ceremony. After they were married, Evins and

Ray lived in the Dyersville community before eventually moving to Steiner.

Steiner, originally named **Fowler**, has an interesting history. John W. McKissick was an early settler in the Bosque County area now known as Steiner. In 1847, Mr. McKissick, a hotel owner in Waco, purchased a league of land between Steele Creek and Cedron Creek for 25 cents an acre. He built a log cabin on the land, but soon returned to Waco because settlers in the Bosque County area were sparse and the danger of Indians was very prominent. The McKissick family returned to Bosque County in 1849.

Another early settler in the Fowler area was Albert Barton. Mr. Barton and his family settled near the junction of Steele Creek and the Brazos River around 1850. Soon after they settled, they built a ferry on the Brazos River near Fort Graham. This ferry carried people from the Bosque County side across the Brazos River to the Hill County side. Not long after Mr. Barton built the ferry, he drowned crossing the Brazos when the ferry capsized due to a sudden rise of the river. A few years later, Mr. Barton's widow married Sam Barnes and they continued to live in the area and operate the ferry on the Brazos River.

In 1869 James Lane bought 1717 acres of land in the James Steele Survey from Jane Gorman Stamps. This land was located north of Steele Creek about a half mile from the Brazos River. Part of this land would eventually be **Fowler, Texas**, later known as **Steiner, Texas**.

Fowler officially became a town with a post office in 1880. The first postmaster of Fowler was Albert McMahan. Also in 1880 the Houston and Texas Central Railroad Company built a railroad line through Fowler. Fowler was a convenient stop on the Houston and Texas Central Railroad that eventually became the Missouri, Kansas and Texas, or Katy Railroad. By 1884 the town of Fowler had an estimated population of fifty. The population may have reached one hundred fifty by 1896.

About the time the railroad name changed to Missouri, Kansas and Texas, someone discovered there was another place in Texas called Fowler. Around 1916 the Postmaster General of the United States was Albert Sidney Burleson. Mr. Burleson's wife, Adele, was Adele Steiner before they got married. Adele's father, Doctor Josephus M. Steiner, was a soldier and post physician at Fort Graham, near Fowler. He owned the Steiner Valley Ranch in Hill County across the Brazos River from

Fowler. He also owned land on the Bosque County side of the Brazos River near Fowler. When a new name was being considered for Fowler, *Steiner* was the name selected by the Postmaster General of the United States. Will Pallmeyer was Postmaster of **Fowler** at the time the name changed to **Steiner** and continued to be Postmaster under the new name.

According to Steiner history, Adele Burleson's sister married C.D. Johns. The two brothers-in-law, C.D. Johns and Albert Burleson, owned a farm adjoining the Steiner depot. There was a convict farm across the Brazos River from the Burleson/ Johns' farm, and men from the convict farm worked the Burleson/Johns' land. Mr. Johns also owned and operated the general store at Steiner. Will Pallmeyer later purchased the general store from Mr. Johns. Mr. Pallmeyer operated the store and was the Postmaster and railroad Stationmaster.

Along with the Steiner general store, there was a post office, a depot, a pump station at which steam engines for the railroad got their water, a second general store, a cotton gin, a blacksmith shop, a garage, a gristmill, two churches, a school, and later, a central telephone office at Steiner. During Steiner's heyday, several freight trains and three passenger trains per day came through there. Many people would board the train at Steiner and ride to Morgan, Walnut Springs, Whitney or other area towns for a picnic or day of shopping before returning to Steiner. Occasionally, they rode the train all the way to Waco to visit family or attend the circus.

The depression hit Steiner with the same vengeance as it hit other places. My parents had not been married long, and later shared with me how they thought they were going to starve to death during those years. My dad worked anywhere he could find work—for long hours and very little pay. One job my daddy had during this time was plowing for a farmer down the road. My dad plowed all day with a team of mules, stopping only to eat a quick dinner and once or twice more during the day to get a drink of water. He started plowing when the sun came up and plowed until it was too dark to see what he was doing. His pay was one dollar for each day that he plowed. My mother told me this dollar often meant the difference between them eating and doing without.

Soon my parents had two more mouths to feed. My oldest sister, Bonnie Ladene, was born February 1, 1931, and my brother, Mearl Odell, was born

September 27, 1932. In order to make a living for his growing family, my dad rented the Steiner general store from Mr. Will Pallmeyer in 1935. Along with my parents operating the general store, my dad was the Postmaster and railroad Stationmaster. He also operated an automobile garage, a gristmill, an icehouse and a feed store. By this time, my daddy had surrendered to preach.

My parents, my sister and brother lived in the back half of the Steiner general store building. My grandparents, J.W. and Leola Cole, known as Ma and Pa to everyone at Steiner, lived in a small apartment added on to the back of the blacksmith shop and gristmill building. Pa operated the blacksmith shop and helped with the gristmill and feed store. Since the Steiner store and all the outbuildings were within a stone's throw of each other, Ma and Pa were a big part of my family's life. My mother worked in the store, washed, ironed, cleaned, cooked and did all the things expected of a wife and mother, so Ma often shared these duties with my mother. The two of them soon had a new task. My Christmas sister, Barbara Ann, was born on December 25, 1938 in the family living quarters behind the Steiner general store.

As the decade of the thirties neared its end, the

depression was not getting much better. To make matters worse, World War II began in 1939. While Adolf Hitler and the German army terrorized much of Europe, the United States had not yet entered the war. Even so, war was definitely on the horizon. In the midst of world chaos, on September 15, 1940, I was born in our living quarters behind the Steiner store. On September 16, 1940, one day after I was born, President Franklin Roosevelt signed into law the Selective Service Act. This act required men age twenty-one to thirty-five to register for the draft. Women did not have to register for the draft; however, they could enlist in the Armed Forces as WAC's, WAVE's, WAF's and SPARS.

On December 7, 1941 Japan's early morning attack on Pearl Harbor plunged the United States into war. During the nearly two-hour assault on Pearl Harbor, Japanese aircraft sank eighteen American ships, destroyed one hundred seventy-four American planes and killed or wounded over three thousand people. Following this attack, many other Americans lost their lives in World War II. Finally, on September 2, 1945, three years, eight months and twenty-six days after Japan bombed Pearl Harbor, General Douglas MacArthur, under the direction of U.S. President, Harry Truman, signed a peace treaty with Japan. This peace treaty, signed aboard the battleship *Missouri* in Tokyo Bay, signified Japan's surrender and marked the end of the war.

World War II took its toll on the United States and on Steiner, Texas. Times were hard during the 1940's. Food items, gasoline, tires and other things were scarce, and people were issued ration books to use for purchasing the necessities. War Bonds helped finance the war. Families struggled to make a living. A new automobile cost around seven hundred dollars, but no one at Steiner had seven hundred dollars. It was hard enough to scrounge up eighteen cents for a gallon of gasoline or eight cents for a loaf of bread. A gallon of milk cost less than fifty cents, but people at Steiner did not buy milk. Most families had a cow for their milk and a few chickens they used for eggs or an occasional meal of fried chicken. Beans were staple items in those days.

I was just over a year old when the United States entered World War II and not quite five years old when the war ended. As a young child, I really did not understand what war meant. Though times were very hard, my parents made sure our family had food to eat and clothes to wear. It did not bother me that my clothes were made from feed sacks because all the children I knew wore clothes made from feed sacks. It also was a reality that most of the clothes I wore had already been worn and outgrown by one or both of my older sisters. Since I was the baby of the family, when I outgrew the clothes, my mother salvaged usable parts of the garments for a quilt top. On very rare occasions, I remember selecting the particular feed sack for my mother to use to make me a new dress. This dress was extra special to me, in that it was mine and mine alone, and had not been worn, outgrown and passed down to me. New shoes were a luxury that few families in Steiner could afford. Our summer months were spent running barefoot.

One thing that remains in my mind, is that although I did not have many clothes, and the clothes I had were made from feed sacks, my mother had a thing about cleanliness. Water was a scarce commodity in those days, but we bathed regularly. My mother scrubbed us until she must have scrubbed at least a layer of skin from our bodies. The dresses I wore were clean and ironed. My black patent Sunday shoes were freshly shined with a leftover biscuit. I had a Sunday dress or two and shoes to wear to church. When I got home from church, my mother made sure I pulled the Sunday dress and shoes off, and put on an everyday dress before I went outside to play.

The Cole family was no worse off than anyone else during those early years of my life. Despite how bad times were, we always had plenty to eat. It was helpful that my daddy ran a grocery store. More than that, God was good to our family and provided enough for us and some left over to share with those less fortunate than we were.

- 2 -

My Birth and Early Life

Come rain, shine, sleet or snow, my parents were in church anytime the doors opened; however, this day was an exception. My mother had a mission to accomplish, and the mission kept her out of church. Knowing my mother, she no doubt met this responsibility much like she met all others in her life—with determination, perseverance and a will to succeed. I can personally testify that my mother's mission was a success. I am living proof of this. At 5:45 a.m., Sunday, September 15, 1940 my mother joined forces with Doctor LaCroix to bring me into this world. My first glimpse of my new world was inside the humble living quarters behind Steiner store. These four rooms welcomed me with my first cry and were my home for the next nine years of my life.

I was the fourth child born to my parents, Evins and Ray Cole. When I was born, my oldest sister, Bonnie, was almost ten years old. My lone brother, Mearl, was a few days shy of his eighth birthday. Barbara would celebrate her second birthday on Christmas Day, December 25, 1940.

On the day I was born, Hank Williams Senior celebrated his seventeenth birthday. Gene Autry, Roy Rogers and Ronald Reagan were popular movie stars during this time. The December 1939 movie, "Gone With the Wind," starring Clark Gable as "Rhett Butler" and Vivien Leigh as "Scarlett O'Hara" was very popular. Rhett's line from the movie, "Frankly, my dear..." would be quoted for years to come. Of course, Steiner folks knew little of movies and movie stars. Their main concern was to put food on the table for their families. They had little or no money left over for frills.

From what I understand, my parents had an argument the day I was born over what to name me. Both of them liked the name "Shirley" and agreed on that for my first name. My daddy wanted to name me "Shirley Temple Cole," but my mother did not like that name. They finally agreed on "Shirley Glenda Cole" as my full name. I always felt sad that my daddy did not win that argument. As a small child, I remember fantasizing that if my name were "Shirley Temple Cole," I would be a star who could sing and dance like Shirley Temple. That was quite a fantasy because I have never been able to carry a tune. As for the dancing part, my strict, Baptist-preacher daddy did not allow his children to dance.

My sister, Bonnie, loved her new baby sister. She carried me around and was a little mother to me. My brother, Mearl, was hoping for a boy and was unimpressed with a new baby sister. Barbara had been the baby for less than two years and, apparently, was not ready to give up her prestigious position in the family. For the first seventeen years of my life, Barbara and I had one long, continual battle over toys, clothes, cars, boys and anything else we could find to fight about. I am happy to say we got past that a long time ago. Barbara, Bonnie and I have shared a close relationship as sisters and friends for many years!

I have heard a story about my early life that I doubt, though several family members, including my mother, shared the story with me. As the story goes, when I was little I nursed a bottle like any other normal baby, but I continued to nurse my bottle until almost time for me to start to school. Family members have further enhanced this story.

Bonnie said she attempted to get me to quit nursing my bottle by reminding me I was about to start to school and would be ashamed if I had to take my bottle with me. This did not work. Then Bonnie refused to fix my bottle for me, but this did not deter me either. I fixed my own bottle and hid behind a certain door in the house to nurse the bottle. Finally, my mother called upon my daddy to exercise his head-of-the-household authority and take my bottle away from me. Since my daddy took this responsibility quite seriously, he set about to solve the problem and handled the situation in his usual, gentle manner. He announced to the family that if I wanted to take my bottle to school with me that was okay!

I was almost seven years old the summer before I started to school. My first grade year would be Bonnie's senior year and she did not want to be embarrassed by her baby sister bringing a bottle to school. She decided it was time to take the situation into her own hands. She finally broke me from my bottle by telling me she threw the bottle in the pigpen. I did quit nursing my bottle, and at the same time, I quit drinking milk. This was due in part to me being very mad at the pigs for taking my bottle. I do remember finding my bottle hidden away several years later. When I found the bottle, I was mad at Bonnie instead of the pigs, but I soon got over my anger. Even though I was no longer mad, I never did start drinking milk again.

I am a close friend with memories from my childhood. Most of these memories are good ones; however, some are not good. While we lived at Steiner, my parents did their best to shield Barbara and me from sadness and death. At times, this was not possible.

Will and Verna Pallmeyer and their son, William, lived next door to the Steiner store in the direction of Steiner Church. William was involved in a very bad car accident and the doctors were not sure he would live. I remember people in our church praying for William and the Pallmeyer family. It did not matter that the Pallmeyer's were Methodist. When someone in a small, close-knit community like Steiner had a problem, everyone felt the pain. After several weeks in the hospital, William did survive and lived in Meridian with his wife, Maleta, until his death in July 2007.

Mrs. Wallace lived in a small house past the Pallmeyer's house. By the time she became my friend, she was an older widow, but her proud, erect stature belied her years. Mrs. Wallace wore simple, yet immaculate, dresses and pulled her white hair into a knot at the back of her head. Her husband, James M. Wallace, died July 26, 1928 when he fell from the top of the Steiner Baptist Church brush arbor while it was under construction.

Occasionally, I walked down to Mrs. Wallace's house to visit her. Her house was like most houses in the Steiner area, an unpretentious board house that had seen no paint. The living room, though clean, was scantily furnished. A chair and table were just inside the door near the only window in the room. An open Bible lay on the table. One could tell by looking at the worn Bible that Mrs. Wallace used it often. The front bedroom was the interesting room in Mrs. Wallace's house. This had been her son's room before he died. It was exactly as he left it the day he went off to war. Mrs. Wallace allowed me to go in the room and look around, but she cautioned me not to touch anything. When she talked about her dead husband and son it was as if they were still alive. There was no bitterness or self-pity, just acceptance for her solitary lot in life.

Mrs. Wallace was a devout Christian and faithful member of Steiner Baptist Church. She was there every time the church doors opened. It was a sad day for me when I heard that Mrs. Wallace died.

I knew she was older, but I had never considered the possibility that, one day, she would not be there at her house just down the road. One thing I remember about Mrs. Wallace is that she was always happy to see me when I went to visit her. She was my friend, and took time to talk and listen to me. The world would be a much better place if there were more people like Mrs. Wallace who went out of her way to befriend a child.

My great-grandparents, Bluford and Martha (King) Allen, lived down a sandy lane off the main Steiner road. Their house was very near the Brazos River just past where Les and Zola Mae Webb and their family lived. I never knew my great-grandfather as he died in January 1936, four years before I was born. According to my mother, it had been cold and rainy for several days before his death. The road in front of the Steiner store was normally a dusty, dirt road, but with all the rain, it was a muddy, dirt road. The sandy lane leading to my great-grandparents' house was practically impassable. When the hearse from Lomax Funeral Home in Meridian came for my great-grandfather's body, the driver could not go down the muddy road to his house. Family members brought his body in a wagon from the house to the main road and helped transfer the body from the wagon to the waiting hearse.

I remember going to see my great-grandmother Allen several times during the years after my great-grandfather died. As a child, I was impressed with the sandy lane and sandy front yard of her house. The back yard of the house was quite different. Instead of sand, large rocks covered this part of the yard. These rocks led to a steep bluff overlooking the Brazos River. When we went to my great-grandmother's, I loved to play on the big rocks in her back yard. One day I was playing on the rocks with several other children. Suddenly one of the children screamed and ran toward the house. A huge rattlesnake, coiled and ready to strike, was on one of the rocks near where we were playing. An adult came out of the house and killed the snake with a hoe. This was the end of our playtime on the rocks!

My mother's uncle, Doug Smith, got a new puppy. One day, Doug and the puppy were playing and the puppy bit Doug on the hand. At the time, the puppy seemed to be okay. Soon Doug got very sick and died of hydrophobia, now called rabies. Bonnie and Mearl, along with my parents, had ridden in the car with Doug shortly before he died. My parents carried Bonnie and Mearl to Doctor

Burnet in Kopperl. Doctor Burnet thought Bonnie and Mearl should take rabies shots since they were so young. They started the daily, painful shots in the stomach. Finally, a communication came from Austin informing my parents that unless the dog bit Bonnie and Mearl, they did not have to take the shots. By this time, they were almost through with the series of shots.

If people in the Steiner area needed a doctor, they had few choices. Doctor Cicero Faulkner was an early doctor in Steiner. He lived in what once had been the Steiner Methodist Church. The building was remodeled into a residence and office for Doctor Faulkner. Doctor Faulkner married Betty Turner, sister of J.E. Turner who owned Turner Drug in Meridian. After Doctor and Mrs. Faulkner moved to Whitney, Doctor Cooper lived in the house vacated by the Faulkner's. By the late 1930's, there was not a doctor living at Steiner. If someone needed a doctor, a family member went to the doctor's office in a nearby town and brought the doctor back to their home. Doctor Burnet lived in Kopperl and helped many Steiner families through sicknesses and childbirths. Doctor Treat lived in Whitney, which was in Hill County. When it was time for Bonnie to be born, Uncle Lois, my daddy's brother, went by wagon to the railroad bridge that separated Bosque County from Hill County. Doctor Treat came from Whitney in his wagon and walked across the railroad trestle spanning the Brazos River to where Uncle Lois was waiting. Uncle Lois carried Doctor Treat by wagon to where my parents lived. Bonnie was born soon after Doctor Treat arrived.

Prior to my birth, Doctor Burnet retired from his medical practice in Kopperl, and Doctor LaCroix replaced him. Doctor LaCroix gave me my first spanking when I was only a few seconds old.

When Steiner folks died, a family member came to the Steiner store and used the only telephone in Steiner to call J.T. Lomax Funeral Home in Meridian. Someone from the funeral home came for the deceased person, took them for embalmment and prepared the body for burial. Later, funeral home personnel brought the body, in the casket, back to the person's home. Family members and friends sat by the casket all night. The funeral was usually the next day in a Steiner-area church. Before the funeral, the casket was transported to the church by a funeral home hearse. My daddy preached many of these funerals. Most often, burial was in the Steiner, Cedron, Kopperl or Morgan Cemetery.

- 3 -

Surviving the Lean Years

My parents worked hard to feed and care for their family. In the 1940's, a woman's place was in the home raising the children and tending to the different homemaking duties. My mother's place was in the home raising the children, tending to the different homemaking duties, helping run the Steiner store, working in the cotton fields, or whatever else she had to do to help make a living. Thankfully, Ma Cole helped out a lot; otherwise, there would not have been enough of my mother to go around.

We ate our family meals at a round, oak table in the kitchen. Breakfast was "breakfast," the noon meal was "dinner," and the evening meal was "supper". Our day started off right with a wholesome breakfast. We might have oatmeal, homemade biscuits, syrup, homemade jelly or preserves and, in hog killing season, ham, bacon or sausage. We ate this meal, like all our meals, on green plates that were premiums from Quaker Mother's Oats. Our matching cups and saucers also came from oatmeal boxes. One thing I remember about breakfast had to do with the green cups and saucers. After my mother poured my dad's hot coffee into one of these cups with the saucer underneath, my daddy poured some coffee from the cup into the saucer. Then he would blow on the coffee until it was cool enough to drink and drink it from the saucer.

For dinner, my mother always cooked a large pone of cornbread in her heavy, iron skillet. Most days we had red beans to go with the cornbread; however, sometimes my mother cooked butter beans, white navy beans, lima beans or black-eyed peas instead. A small hunk of salt pork simmered in the pot with the beans to give them extra flavor. Along with beans and cornbread, my mother might cook fried potatoes, Polk salad, corn on the cob, turnips and greens, sweet potatoes or other vegetables, and some kind of dessert. Our drink was iced tea. My mother believed in making her tea strong and sweet. She boiled the loose leaves several times to be sure she got as much tea as she could out of them. Though she made tea daily, we always had to drink "yesterday's tea" before we could drink the tea she made that day. The left-over tea was even stronger and sweeter than the tea made fresh that day. My mother's tea is the reason I never developed a love for tea. If she or Bonnie would have filled my bottle with tea, that probably would have broken me from nursing my bottle.

During the week, my mother never knew how many people she was cooking for. Besides our family, someone might be at the store waiting to catch the train or to have their car repaired. When my daddy came to dinner, he brought the guests to the house to eat with our family. For this reason, my mother always cooked extra food. No matter how many people were there at mealtime, there was enough food for everyone and leftovers for the evening meal.

When my daddy came to the house to eat, he followed a ritual. A bucket of water with a ladle sat on the kitchen drain. My dad poured a ladle of water into a small pan sitting by the bucket. Then he pulled off his hat, wet his comb, combed his hair, washed his face and hands and came to the table. The table was set in the usual country fashion with the plates turned upside down. As we sat down at the table, we all bowed our heads and my daddy asked the blessings. As a small child I remember thinking my daddy was reading his prayer from the writing on the bottom of the plates. After the blessings, plates were turned upright and bowls of food passed around the table.

Our Sunday meal was the same, yet different. Most of the meal was prepared on Saturday and completed early Sunday morning before we went to church. My mother often fried two or more chickens that she killed and dressed herself. Along with the fried chicken, we had many of the same vegetables that we had during the week, and some kind of dessert. My mother liked to cook pies and it was not unusual for us to have three or four different kinds of pies at the same meal.

In the summertime, my mother canned vegetables, grape and plum juice, peaches, blackberries and other fruits. This canning was done in a pressure cooker on an old wood stove, so with summer heat, the kitchen often felt like an inferno. The only cooling came from a small, oscillating fan sitting in the kitchen floor. There was no waiting until the weather was cooler to do the canning. The availability set the pace for canning, and fruits and vegetables were canned as they ripened. Later my mother made jelly from the grape and plum juice and canned the jelly. In the wintertime, our family reaped the benefits of summer canning. My mother often opened one of the jars of fruit and made a big cobbler with thick, homemade crust on the top. Nothing tasted better than a juicy cobbler made from one of the jars of fruit my mother canned during the summer.

Washing clothes was a weekly occurrence at our house. Monday was washday, and the day started early with my mother outside building a roaring fire under her big, black wash pot. Three large tubs sat side-by-side on a crude, homemade workbench next to the wash pot. My mother sorted the dirty clothes into three piles: white clothes, colored clothes and work clothes. A rub board, bars of homemade lye soap, a pan of stiff starch made by cooking flour and water together, an old broom handle and a bottle of bluing sat on the workbench.

My mother put the white clothes in one tub, covered them with boiling water from the wash pot and allowed them to soak for a few minutes. Sheets were first, followed by other white clothes. After the clothes soaked, she scrubbed them on the rub board with lye soap. My mother was a stickler for white clothes looking white, so after she rubbed and wrung them, she put them in the boiling water in the wash pot. She punched them up and down with the broom handle until any remaining dirt and stubborn stains disappeared. She then used the broom handle to lift each piece from the boiling water in the wash pot. After they dripped free of dirty water she put them in the rinse tub. When she felt the pieces were rinsed properly, she wrung them once again and transferred them to the third tub, the bluing tub. After a final hand wringing, she hung the clothes on the clothes' line to dry.

My mother repeated most of the steps above for the colored clothes and work clothes. Since my dad's work clothes were greasy from working on cars, my mother soaked them in gasoline first. Then she rinsed them in a tub of used rinse water to get the gasoline off. She did all of this before she started washing the work clothes. Before the day was over, my mother used countless buckets of water previously hauled from the creek. Bonnie helped with the washing and with hauling water. Luckily, Barbara and I were still considered too young to help.

Washday was a tedious process of scrubbing, punching, wringing, rinsing, bluing and hanging clothes. Sunday clothes required an extra step of starching and wringing before they were hung to dry. There were never enough lines for all the clothes and some were spread across barbed wire fences to dry.

Clothes had to be washed weekly despite the weather. If it rained Monday, washday was Tuesday. Hot weather or cold weather was not a reason to change washday. My mother washed outside in an air-conditioned and heated area next to the smokehouse. The only problem was, Mother Nature controlled the thermostat; therefore, it was extremely hot in the summer and equally cold in the winter.

Ironing day followed washday. Unlike washing, ironing was done indoors because it required a stove to heat the irons. My mother started ironing right after breakfast while the wood stove was still hot. An iron in those days was exactly what its name said, five to seven pounds of solid iron. My mother ironed with one iron while two or three others heated on top of the wood stove. She might use two irons to iron a shirt or dress and three irons for my dad's heavy pants. Since the irons had to be red hot, hardly an ironing day went by without burned hands. If dirt or soot from the wood stove got on the iron, it usually transferred to the garment. This was especially disastrous if my mother was ironing a light-colored dress or one of my daddy's white shirts. The garment had to be washed again.

My mother ironed on a homemade, wooden ironing board that my dad made. Several layers of old sheets covered the board. Occasionally, hot irons scorched and burned holes in the ironing board cover so my mother replaced it often.

Ironing was much harder in the summer than in the winter. Along with the backbreaking labor of lifting the heavy irons all day, the intense heat from the wood stove, combined with the oppressive summer temperatures, made the task almost unbearable. Still, ironing had to be done and my mother was not one to shirk her responsibilities.

President Roosevelt (FDR) established the Rural Electrification Administration in 1935. This agency's responsibility was to oversee the expansion of electric power to people in rural areas of the United States. In 1935 only one household in every ten in the United States had commercial electric service. That one household was not in Steiner, Texas. According to my daddy, Congressman W.R. (Bob) Poage came to the Steiner store and promised to help get electric lines built to supply electricity to folks in Steiner. I do not know when electric power came to the Steiner area, but before that, my daddy developed a delco battery system that supplied electric power for our house and the store. After he did this, my mother had an early version washing machine and electric iron. These modern conveniences made life in the Cole household much easier.

In March 1940 my parents scraped together enough money for a down payment on two hundred fifty acres of land several miles from the Steiner store. This place was known as the "Wallace Place" because James M. and Laura Wallace lived there for many years after they purchased it from Sarah Claybrook. Mr. Wallace died in 1928, and Laura Wallace sold the land to W.C. and Verna Pallmeyer in 1936. My parents bought the place from the Pallmeyer's for eight hundred dollars down and one hundred seventy-five dollars a year for the next nine years, which was nine dollars and fifty cents an acre.

The Wallace Place was an invaluable water source because it had a windmill and cement holding tank. The windmill supplied much of the drinking water hauled to our house. The Lee McCurdy family lived on the Wallace place across the road from the windmill. On the same side of the road as their house, there was a high hill with the old Wallace house on top. The Wallace place had quite a few acres of productive farmland. My dad used some land to graze cows and some to grow crops.

Cotton was one of the crops my dad planted on the Wallace place. He, like other farmers in the Steiner area, used the almanac to know when to plant the cotton. If the summer rains fell just right and boll weevils weren't too bad, the fertile land on the banks of the Brazos River made a good crop of cotton. As September came, so did the impending cotton harvest. My parents picked as much of their cotton themselves as they could. Before I started to school, I went to the cotton field occasionally with my parents. For me, going to the cotton field to pick cotton was an enjoyable experience. This could be because I did not pick much cotton. Probably the longest time I spent picking cotton in a day was fifteen minutes. The rest of the time I played in the cotton on the wagon, rode on my daddy's cotton sack, took a nap under the wagon or amused myself in other ways. I had a small cotton sack my mother made for me. Somehow, my little sack mysteriously was full at the end of the day. I still remember how important I felt when my daddy put a few coins in my hand for my day's pay in the cotton field.

I loved cotton field dinners eaten in the shade of the wagon. Even now I remember everything from that time, down to the smallest detail. My parents' fingers were often bloody from repetitious encounters with sharp cotton bolls, so before we ate, we washed our hands. Next my daddy asked the blessings and thanked God for the food we were about to eat. Then my mother spread the bountiful feast of potted meat, sardines, Vienna sausage, pork and beans, crackers, bread, pickles and maybe a jar of her spiced peaches. My daddy filled metal cups with cool, cistern water from a gallon jug wrapped in a wet burlap bag. Oh, how the cotton field food and cool water tasted to a small child.

I do not think my parents had as much fun as I did picking cotton. They wore thick denim overalls, long sleeved shirts and large straw hats to protect themselves from the sweltering September sun. Homemade leather pads strapped around their knees and gloves that had the fingers cut off completed their uniform. They spent long days in the cotton field dragging bulging cotton sacks up and down rows of cotton that seemed to have no end. When the sacks were full, my parents took them to the wagon parked in the middle of the field, weighed their cotton and heaved the heavy sacks over the side of the wagon. After they emptied the sacks, it was all to do over as they filled and emptied them several times during the day. Bull nettles, scorpions, copper heads and rattle snakes were constant threats in the cotton field. Those dangers, along with sore knees, infected fingers, and aching backs did not stop my parents from going on to the next row of cotton. They stopped only when all the cotton was picked and on the way to the cotton gin in Kopperl or Morgan. Thinking back, I'm almost certain my parents did not have fun picking cotton.

My dad and folks in the Steiner area dipped their cows in the summertime to kill flies and other insects. This dipping took place at a common area near Steele Creek. If you went from the store where we lived past Steiner Baptist Church and crossed the railroad track, you soon came to a low-water crossing over Steele Creek. Just on the other side of this crossing, there was a large, concrete receptacle for dipping cattle. This receptacle was similar to a swimming pool, with openings at each end for the cows to enter and exit. It gradually got deeper in the middle. Everyone in the community who wanted to take part in the cattle dipping pitched in and purchased several gallons of insecticide. Men hauled water the short distance from Steele Creek and filled the deep part of the concrete receptacle. The insecticide was then added to the water in the dipping tank. On cattle dipping day, people drove their cows down the road and into one end of the dipping tank. The cows went through the deep part of the tank, they were "dipped" and then they went out the other end.

To help feed our family, my daddy killed a hog each year in the fall. I do not mean that he actually killed the hog, because my daddy could never kill anything. For this job, my dad had to have outside help from Lee McCurdy. Hog killing day was always a cold, November day. The hog killing area was in the pasture behind our house under a grove of live oak trees. The men prepared for the day starting early in the morning. They filled large wash pots with water and heated them to boiling over open fires. A block and tackle hung from a tree. Razor sharp knives and several barrels were nearby. When everything was ready, Lee shot the hog with a .22 caliber rifle. The men wrapped a chain around the dead hog and raised him to the tree with the block and tackle. Then they lowered the hog into a barrel filled with boiling water. After a while, they removed the hog from the barrel with the block and tackle, suspended him from the tree and began the tedious job of scraping the hair off the hog's body. My daddy poured more scalding water on the hog to wash the loose hairs off. Then my dad and Lee used the sharp knives to gut the hog, skin the carcass and butcher the animal. The skin and layer of fat just inside the skin were cooked in a big wash pot to render the lard. My mother would use this lard later for cooking and making lye soap. The fat that did not cook away into lard was made into cracklings. These cracklings were good eaten fresh and they also made delicious crackling cornbread. Lee and my dad trimmed bacon, hams and other choice hog meat to perfection. The bacon and hams were cured and would keep for a while. Some of the meat was ground into sausage, my mother made sausage patties and fried them. After they were fried, she alternated layers of sausage with thin layers of lard and stored them in large cans. Prepared in this fashion, the sausage would keep for a few weeks. With no refrigeration, the fresh meat had to be eaten within a few days. The McCurdy family received part of the meat for Lee's help with the hog butchering.

During the war, securing food and other items was a bit more complicated with the introduction of President Roosevelt's rationing program. People had to use government issued *War Ration Books* **and** money to buy items. Along with our family's personal rationing books, my dad, a storeowner, had extra responsibilities. He had to mark the correct number of points on tires, food and other items. When customers redeemed their ration stamps, my dad pasted the stamps on gummed sheets and gave the sheets to the wholesaler. This allowed my dad to replenish the rationed items in the store. The wholesaler then turned in his stamps at the bank to get credit to buy more food. Food rationing was a bureaucratic nightmare!

In September 1945 my dad bought one hundred-fifteen additional acres of land adjoining the Wallace place. He bought this land from the Yates' family heirs for three thousand, four hundred ninety-eight dollars and seventy-five cents, roughly thirty dollars an acre. My dad ran quite a few cows on the total acreage of three hundred sixty-five acres.

My dad bought a grocery store in Morgan from W.M. Wiley in May of 1946. Bonnie and my mother ran this store while my dad, Ma, Pa and Mearl held down the fort at Steiner. I liked to go to Morgan with my mother and Bonnie and spend the day at the store. On very rare occasions, I remember going to the Morgan Star Theater to see a movie.

The Morgan store was profitable; however, the responsibility for two stores began to wear on the Cole family. Fortunately a buyer came along and purchased the Morgan store. My dad apparently did not learn a lesson from trying to run two stores. In November 1946 he bought the old Kopperl State Bank building from H.M. Gilbert and opened a grocery store in Kopperl. Lee McCurdy and Odell Steen operated this store. Kopperl already had the John Thompson grocery store, the Walter Day grocery store and a general store owned by Floyd "Sleepy" Hill. My dad soon realized the Kopperl population would not support another grocery store. This time he was less fortunate because no one wanted to buy the Kopperl store. In the end, my dad sold the merchandise and closed the store. Eventually, he was able to sell the building.

These years were lean times for my parents and others of their generation. Day after day, my parents and others continued on without complaining. It was no easy existence, but they spent the years doing what they learned early—

making do with whatever they had, never wasting anything and working hard to keep their families from starving.

- 4 -

Steiner Store

By the 1940's Steiner was nothing more than a wide spot in a dusty, gravel road. There was no town, just a community with the Steiner store, surrounding out buildings and a few houses scattered up and down the road. The store at Steiner was the only grocery store in the area. Many people had moved to Kopperl, Morgan, Meridian or other area towns. Lake Whitney was in the planning stages. Steiner was in the flood plain so more and more people were moving away.

Just thinking about the Steiner store and the surrounding buildings brings so many memories to my mind. I summons these memories often, and when I do, I always feel a strange combination of sadness and joy. I can see the store now almost sixty years after it is no longer there.

The store building was an unpainted board building that had weathered none too well through the years. It was not an attractive or impressive building by today's standards; however, it was impressive to a small child in the 1940's. Walk with me on a journey through the Steiner store that started when I was a toddler and ended nine years later when my family moved from Steiner.

Two gasoline pumps stood at the very front of the store building. One pump contained white gasoline; the other pump contained red gasoline. A gallon of the red gasoline costs a few cents more than a gallon of the white. Automobiles and other gasoline engines of the day burned either type. My daddy was a strong advocate for Magnolia brand gasoline. The Magnolia emblem, a flying red horse, proudly hung on a pole at the front of the Steiner store.

A long, wooden, front porch extended all the way across the front of the store building. This porch was several feet off the ground. The porch had a front step and steps on either side that were nothing more than large rocks. I remember a few straight-back wooden chairs sitting on the porch. Often, the people sitting in these chairs had nothing better to do. In the 1940's there were many folks in Steiner,

Texas, who fit this category. A square, metal barrel containing kerosene sat on the left side of the porch. The barrel was probably four feet high and had a pump with a hose attached. When someone needed kerosene, they brought their cans with them to the store and purchased a gallon or two of the liquid. Kerosene was an essential item in those days for lamps and for starting fires in wood stoves.

My sister, Barbara, recently reminded me of an incident involving kerosene and the front porch of the Steiner store. When I was around four or five and Barbara was twenty-one months older, the two of us were playing at the front of the Steiner store. I got interested in something and was bent over intently looking under the porch. Barbara was standing on the porch watching me and noticed a can that she thought had water in it. She contemplated how funny it would be to pour the water on me, so she picked up the can and dumped the contents on my head. Instead of water, the can contained kerosene and I was drenched with the liquid. The kerosene took my breath away and I fell to the ground and lay there lifeless. For a few seconds, Barbara thought she had killed me. Finally I started crying, and my dad came from inside the store to see what was wrong. When he found out Barbara had poured kerosene on my head, he did not think it was funny at all.

As you walked up onto the porch of the Steiner store, there was a wooden, front door leading into the building. Most of the time, this door was opened back against the wall. A screen door, displaying a Mrs. Baird's bread advertisement, kept flies and animals from entering uninvited. When one crossed the threshold into the Steiner store, one stepped into another world. This was a simplistic world, yet a wonderful world when seen through the eyes of a small child.

Inside, the store was one large room with high ceilings, exposed rafters, wooden floors and board walls. Shelves lined many of these walls. The building was well heated and well cooled. It was *heated* in the summertime and *cooled* in the winter, as the building had no heat or air conditioning. In those days, people were not accustomed to comfort so it did not really matter if the building was hot in the summer and cold in the winter. People came to the store to buy essential items and felt really fortunate if they had money to buy them. Sometimes they did not have enough money to pay for groceries or gasoline, but that did not matter either. My dad allowed them to have what they needed on the credit. He kept credit books with people's names on them, and wrote down the date and amount of groceries or gasoline they bought on the credit that day. These credit books were kept in a homemade wooden box under the store counter. Later when the person's cotton came in or when they sold a cow or pig, they came to the store and paid my dad some, or all, of what they owed. Steiner folks accepted responsibility for their debts. My dad trusted them to pay what they owed and most of them did not betray that trust.

I have a 1949 credit book from the Steiner store that has some interesting prices in it. A package of cigarettes cost twenty cents, as did a loaf of bread. Four-ten gauge shotgun shells were eight cents each. Oil was fifteen cents a quart and gasoline twenty-four cents a gallon. A soft drink and bar of candy cost five cents each.

A long, glass, display case was just inside the front door on the right. This case was probably ten feet long and filled with items of yesteryear. The first few feet of the display case held envelopes, pencils, writing tablets, needles for hand sewing and quilting, thread, thimbles, treadle sewing machine needles and belts and small cans of sewing machine oil. There were work socks, suspenders, gloves, combs, round bars of shaving soap, shaving cups and brushes, straight razors, boxes of face powder, bobby pins, hair nets, handkerchiefs for men and ladies and other small staple items. If you needed something from this case, you bought what was there with very little choice. The socks or gloves might not be the right size, but they were the best available.

As a small child, I was not interested in the items in the first area of the glass case. I spent most of my time in the part occupied by beautifully displayed boxes of candy and gum. There were Baby Ruth's, Butterfingers, Almond Joys, Mounds, Hershey bars with or without almonds, Milky Ways, Snickers, peanut butter logs, jaw breakers, Tootsie Rolls, Bubble Gum and several boxes of Juicy Fruit, Spearmint and Double Mint gum. Boxes of Cracker Jacks with much-coveted prizes were displayed behind the candy and gum. Small, cylinder-shaped boxes of peanuts sat next to the Cracker Jacks. If you bought one of these boxes, and if you were very lucky, the box might contain peanuts *and* a paper-wrapped penny or nickel. Even if you did not find money in these peanuts, they were really, really good to eat with a cold soft drink, or soda water as we called it. There was a special way you prepared the soda water and peanuts. After you drank a few sips of the soda water, you poured the box of peanuts into the bottle. With each sip of soda water you got an extra bonus of a few peanuts in your mouth. Just reflecting back on how this delicacy tasted—sweet with a touch of salty—makes my mouth water.

Most items in the candy case sold for a few pennies or no more than five cents, but of course, I could have anything I wanted without paying. Ah, I can still remember how good those chocolate bars tasted and how big they were. My favorite candy was a Hershey bar with almonds. I remember once I ate so many that I got sick and threw up. I do not think I have eaten one since that time.

Luden brand cough drops were also in the candy case. When I think about these cough drops, I remember Leona Williams and her youngest child, Jerry Wayne, coming to the Steiner store. Jerry Wayne would go to the candy case and stand looking at all the candy and gum inside. Then he would tell his mother he wanted some Luden cough drops. These were the original yellow Ludens and not the cherry kind of later years. Leona would try to talk him out of the cough drops, but Jerry Wayne had his mind made up and there was no changing it. If Leona told Jerry Wayne he could not have the cough drops, he would fall in the floor and start crying. He would cry until he got the cough drops and would eat most of them before he left the store.

There were no grocery baskets to push from aisle to aisle in the store. In fact, there were no aisles, just shelves along the walls. Cans or boxes of sardines, salmon, pork and beans, crackers, lard, flour, sugar, oatmeal and other staple items were on the shelves. Shoppers hand-carried a few items at a time to the check out counter located near the back of the store, stopping each trip to pass the time of day with the person behind the counter. This counter was a large, rectangular area with a cash register sitting near the middle of the front section. A scale, with iron weights to balance the weight of the purchase, was nearby for weighing bulk items. Shelves lined the lower front of the check out counter. These shelves had plug tobacco, Bull Durham, Prince Albert and packages of cigarette papers for rolling cigarettes. There were also boxes of Four Way and Bromine cold tablets, Bayer aspirin, bottles of Percy, Castor Oil and other home remedies on the shelves. Glass shades and wicks for kerosene lamps, bottles of bluing, bars of soap and boxes of washing powder lined the shelves behind the counter. Open barrels of red beans and butter beans were near the counter area. There were boxes of Irish potatoes and sometimes sweet potatoes in this area. In the hot summertime, potatoes did not last long. I can still remember the smell of a rotten potato that had gone unnoticed for too long in the hot store.

Thinking about potatoes reminds me of a story about my daddy and how he could not pass up a bargain. We were on the way to Fort Worth to visit my mother's sister and husband, Velma and C.W. Potts, and my mother's brother and family, Leonard, Eula Mae, Jean, Jerry and Don. We treasured these trips to Fort Worth as they were few and far between. My parents and Bonnie were in the front seat of our non-air conditioned car while Barbara, Mearl and I rode in the back. All of us were anxious to get to Fort Worth. Barbara and I especially looked forward to playing with our cousins. Going to Fort Worth also meant our parents would take us to the old Montgomery Wards store on Seventh Street to shop. This was one of the highlights of a trip to Fort Worth.

On the way to Fort Worth, my dad saw a roadside stand advertising one hundred pounds of potatoes for four dollars. He stopped and bought a sack of the potatoes. As we drove a little further, my dad saw another sign advertising one hundred pounds of potatoes for three dollars. Again, he stopped and bought a sack of potatoes. By this time, Bonnie, Mearl, Barbara and I were restless and ready to get to Fort Worth. A few miles down the road, my dad saw another sign advertising one hundred pounds of potatoes for two dollars. Of course, he stopped and bought another sack of potatoes. Even my mother was beginning to complain at this point. She asked my daddy what in the world he was going to do with three hundred pounds of potatoes.

My dad said, "Ray, I just could not pass them up. Don't you see? If I had only bought the first sack, they would have cost me four cents a pound. Now after I bought all three sacks, they just cost me three cents a pound."

Several weeks later, many of the potatoes were rotten and had to be thrown away. My mother was in the store the day my daddy went through the box of potatoes and discarded the rotten ones. With a smile on her face, she could not resist asking my dad what the potatoes cost him then.

Work items were on the back left side of the store building. Articles found in this section were used tires, tubes, cold patch glue, claw hammers, nails, bolts, cotton sack material, brooms, mops, rakes, hoes, mouse traps, fly swatters, chains, ropes and other useful and necessary objects.

People of all ages loved the Steiner store. It did not matter that milk, ice cream, butter, sour cream, yogurt, frozen pizza, T.V. dinners, eggs and other refrigerated items were not sold. There was no refrigeration at the Steiner store. Movies were not available to rent, but this was okay because no one had televisions or recorders to view the movies. Disposable diapers were unheard of. People used old cup towels or other soft cloth for diapers. Sacks of dog or cat food were not on display. If Steiner folks had a dog or cat, they fed them table scraps, not fancy, gourmet pet food. For adults, a trip to the Steiner store was a necessity. It also was a part of their social life. Children loved the candy counter. It was a special treat for them to have a few pennies to spend on candy or gum. They never got much, but they never expected much.

My daddy was the last Postmaster and railroad Ticket Master at Steiner. The post office and railroad ticket office were on the left just inside the front door of the store. Walls that went half way to the ceiling divided this area from the rest of the store. There was a small window opening where people bought stamps, mailed a letter, asked for their mail or bought a train ticket. A small scale for weighing letters sat near the window. Inside the combination post office and ticket office area, a blackboard with train schedules written in chalk leaned against one wall. A few posters hung limply within view. One poster that I remember had a picture of a man dressed in red, white and blue. The man was pointing his finger directly toward the person looking at the poster. The caption, "Uncle Sam Wants You," was written underneath the man's picture.

In the early days, mail came to and from Steiner by train. Before the train arrived, my dad bagged up the outgoing mail and hung the bags on a pole beside the railroad track. As the train came through Steiner, someone on the train grabbed the mailbag off the pole with a special hook. This process went smoothly most of the time; however, there were times when the hook hit the mailbag wrong and mail scattered everywhere. When this happened, the train continued on down the track beside the scattered mail. After the train passed, my dad gathered the mail from beside the railroad track, put it in a new burlap bag and placed the bag back on the pole to await the next train. Incoming mail came by train also. An employee on the train threw burlap bags of mail from the train as it slowly passed through Steiner. These bags were picked up, carried to the post office inside the Steiner store and sorted. Eventually mail came to Steiner by rural carriers instead of by train. One rural mailman that I remember was Mr. Tucker from Meridian.

At one time there was a depot building by the railroad tracks in front of the Steiner store. Bonnie and Mearl remember the depot. I have a picture of Ma and Pa Cole and me when I was around two years old. The depot is in the background of this picture; however, I do not remember the depot building. I recently asked my brother, Mearl, about the depot and he said he thought someone tore it down or moved it from Steiner after it was no longer in use. As far back as I remember, the railroad ticket office shared quarters with the post office in the Steiner store building. I remember people coming to the ticket office to buy tickets to ride the train. Usually they had a small bag with them that contained their traveling clothes. This was not a fancy piece of luggage. It was just a bag sometimes held together with a small rope or string.

The train stopped at Steiner from time to time to let a passenger off. Sometimes they might wait at the Steiner store for several hours for a family member to come pick them up. There was no café at Steiner, so if they were there at mealtime, my daddy invited them to eat with our family. At times, people coming in on the train might not have a ride, so my daddy took them to where they needed to go. When my sister, Bonnie, was no older than eight years old, she cut her driving teeth and often was the designated chauffer in charge of carrying these people to their destinations.

There was an old crank-type telephone in the post office area of the Steiner store. You could call Meridian and talk for three minutes for ten cents. You could not make local calls because the telephone in the store was the only telephone in Steiner. Often, Steiner folks came to the store to use the telephone to make necessary calls. Other times, people called the store long distance and asked my dad to deliver a message to someone in the Steiner area. This message might be that a member of their family was very ill, or maybe even a death message. My daddy or Bonnie delivered this message in person.

My journey through the Steiner store building has now come full-circle. I would dearly love to take that journey one more time. If I could walk through the store again, I would walk very slowly. I would soak in the sights, sounds, and smells and take time to touch things. I would be in no rush to grow up and leave the simple pleasures of my childhood in Steiner, Texas.

- 5 -

My Home

I have previously written that I was born at home. Home for the first nine years of my life was inside the cramped living quarters joined on to the back of the Steiner store. This area consisted of a living room, kitchen, small bedroom and a larger bedroom. One entered the living room of my home through a door at the very back of the Steiner store. Though not a large room, the living room served as a combination living and sleeping area. Bonnie, Barbara and I slept in the living room. Mearl slept in the small bedroom behind the living room and my parents slept in the larger bedroom on the back of the house. This room was an open porch before my dad closed it in to make a bedroom that we called the sleeping porch. There were several windows in this room, unlike the other rooms in our living quarters. The sleeping porch was the coldest room in the house. In the winter, my parents used lots of heavy quilts to keep from freezing to death. Bonnie, Barbara and I were the lucky ones, as the wood stove was in the middle of the combination living room and our bedroom. This stove was the only source of heat in our house.

The sleeping porch was cold in the winter, but by June, it and other rooms in our house were definitely not cold. Hot Texas summers with no air conditioning and few windows made sleeping miserable. As a solution, our back yard became our bedroom. Each summer, my parents moved the heavy, iron beds outside and covered them with mosquito netting, a type of thin, gauze fabric. At night, we crawled under the mosquito netting and sank into our feather mattresses. I still remember the beauty of those nights as we looked up at the stars and moon and listened to the night sounds before drifting off to sleep. In the morning, there definitely was no chance of oversleeping. My mother's rooster made sure we were up at the crack of dawn.

We did not have a bathroom in our house. There was a one-hole outdoor toilet located some distance behind the house. The chamber pot, a white porcelain enamel pan with handles and lid, rested under the bed for night emergencies. With no indoor bathroom, taking baths was interesting. A number-three galvanized tub was our bathtub. Since our water was hauled from Steele creek, several people in the family might use the same tub of water. Bath water was room temperature in the summertime or heated on the wood stove in the wintertime. When we took our bath, the tub was placed near the wood stove in the living room. This made it convenient for warming the water and also helped us stay warm during and after our baths.

Another activity that took place in the living room was quilting. My mother usually had an unfinished quilt that she was working on, especially in the wintertime when outside activities were somewhat limited. My dad made a quilt frame for my mother out of long pieces of lumber. He drilled holes in the lumber every few inches. The quilt frame was suspended from the ceiling at all four corners with lengths of rope. My mother hand-pieced scraps of material together into a quilt top and gathered other items needed for the quilt. She basted the lining, made from feed sacks or muslin, to the quilt frame. Then she layered cotton batting on top of the lining, put the quilt top over this and secured it to the quilt frame with more basting. She was now ready to start the actual quilting. My grandmother helped my mother quilt as did other ladies in the community. Sometimes the quilt was for our family or for another Steiner family. The ladies sat around the quilt in straight-back wooden chairs quilting, laughing and talking for hours at a time. As work on the quilt progressed, the quilt frame was rolled to the inside and secured with nails put into the holes drilled in the frame. This step was necessary to allow the ladies access to the inner parts of the quilt. A quilt usually took several days to complete. If the quilt was not finished at the end of each evening, the ropes at the four corners of the frame were wrapped around and around the frame until it was up and out of the way. When the ladies were ready to quilt again, the frame was lowered to the desired height and another session of quilting was underway.

The kitchen joined the living room of our home. By today's standards, our kitchen was very primitive. Taking center stage in the kitchen was the large, round, oak table. This table was the nucleus of our family's life. All of our meals were eaten around this table. The table was also where we completed our school-work, where family problems were discussed and where financial books from the store were reconciled.

Of no less importance in the kitchen were the icebox and cook stove. The icebox was just what its name suggested—a wooden "box" that had to have a block of ice inside to keep items cold. Our icebox was made of oak and had three sections. Each section had a separate door with heavy hinges and latches. One area was for the block of ice, another area was for milk and other food items and a smaller area held a pan to catch water from the melting ice.

For most of the nine years that I lived at Steiner, my mother cooked on a wood stove. Sometime before we moved from Steiner in 1949, my dad bought my mother a shiny, white, gas cook stove. You would have thought my dad had given my mother a diamond ring or mink coat. She was so proud of that stove.

The kitchen did not have actual kitchen cabinets. Open shelves held dishes, canned goods and other kitchen items. The room had a small table that my mother used for her baking preparation area. A clean cup towel covered the wooden bread bowl, rolling pin, flour sifter and large mixing bowls that were on top of the table. Shelves, lined with oilcloth, were underneath the table. Flour, meal, sugar, lard, baking powder, soda, salt and other items sat on these shelves. A pie safe, a type of kitchen cabinet with perforated metal doors, sat nearby. The perforations in the doors allowed ventilation for my mother's freshly made pies, cakes and rolls. I can still see my mother standing by the table, a freshly washed and ironed flour-sack apron tied around her waist, painstakingly rolling out piecrust. After my mother rolled the crust into a large circle, she carefully transferred the thin dough onto a metal pan. Then she pressed the crust into the pan, pricked all around the bottom and sides of the dough-covered pan and fluted the edges of the piecrust. Finally, she filled the crust with apples, peaches, apricots, mincemeat, chocolate, coconut, pecan or other homemade fillings, and baked the pies. There was always a pie, cake, homemade rolls or something cooking that made the whole house smell so good.

As I previously mentioned, my mother baked cornbread daily in her black, cast iron skillet. She started by sifting cornmeal and a little flour into a large bowl. Next she opened a wide-mouthed fruit jar that contained salt, and took some salt out of the jar with her hand. She repeated this procedure with another jar that contained soda. She carefully broke a fresh egg, added it to the dry mixture in the bowl and then poured in buttermilk. My mother did not use a recipe or measure any of the ingredients. She just somehow *knew* how much she needed of each item. I watched her make this cornbread often and I always wondered how she determined how much meal or buttermilk to put into the cornbread.

A crude drain board lined one wall of the kitchen. Since the kitchen did not have a built in sink, my mother washed dishes in a white enamel pan on the drain board. A metal water bucket with a dipper hanging on the side sat on the end of the drain board near the kitchen door. When someone wanted a cool drink of water, they used this dipper to drink from and then hung it back on the bucket for the next person to use.

My daddy had a very imaginative, creative mind. This creativity allowed him to develop ways to supply modern conveniences for his family. These ideas were usually ahead of the times. For example, few people in Steiner had running water, but because of my daddy's ingenuity, we *sometimes* had running water. We had a cistern, a large metal tank for catching and storing rainwater, just outside our living quarters. My dad piped water from this cistern into the kitchen, and as I said, we sometimes had running water. More often, we did not. In rainy seasons, we usually had water in the cistern for drinking. Our water for other purposes was hauled from Steele creek or the Wallace place. During dry seasons, Bonnie hauled a load of water every day. If it was washday she might make two trips a day. Once when Bonnie was going to get a load of water, our cousin, Bud Cole, was at our house and wanted to go with her. Since the creek was low, they went to the Wallace place because there was a windmill there. When they got to the Wallace place Bonnie turned the windmill on so the concrete tank could fill with water. Then she dipped buckets of water and poured them into the fifty gallon barrels in the back of the pickup. While Bonnie filled the barrels, Bud sat under a tree. Bonnie told him if he did not help, he was not going to ride back to the store. Apparently, Bud did not believe this, as he continued to sit under the tree. After Bonnie got the barrels filled, she covered them with heavy ducking material and put metal rings around the top of the barrels over the ducking. She then got in the pickup, rolled the windows up, locked the doors and started the motor. Bud came running to get in the cab of the pickup and Bonnie reminded him what she told him about helping her fill the barrels. Bonnie drove a short distance, stopped, and then unlocked the door on the passenger side and told Bud he could ride. By this time, Bud was not too happy and refused to get in the pickup. Bonnie tried to get him to ride several times, but he walked all the way to the Steiner store, a distance of four or five miles.

My mother's storm cellar was near the side door of our house. This storm cellar was nothing fancy. Actually, it was just a dug out hole in the ground reinforced across the top with wooden crossties. Sheets of tin covered the crossties and a dirt roof covered the tin. The cellar had a heavy, wooden door at the front with a rope attached on the inside to hold the door closed during bad windstorms. Packed dirt steps led down into the cellar. My mother was very afraid of storms, so she always kept an eye on the weather. Thinking back, it seems most of the bad storms came in the middle of the night. If a storm was approaching and it started thundering and lightening, my mother woke everyone up. She tried to get my daddy to go to the cellar with the rest of the family, but he would not go. My mother, Bonnie, Mearl, Barbara and I went to the cellar far ahead of the worst of the storm. The cellar had dugout bench beds so we continued our sleep on these hard, dirt-packed beds. Often we encountered snakes or large spiders in the cellar, but my mother always assured us they were harmless. I suspect it was a case of her being less afraid of snakes and spiders than she was of storms. Usually a storm blew over and we returned to the house after an hour or two. At times, the storm got more severe with lots of wind and hard rain. If this happened, at some point, my daddy would become frightened. He would grab one of my mother's best quilts off the bed and head for the cellar. During one really bad storm, my dad ran for the cellar, dragging the quilt through the rain puddles all the way. The wind was blowing hard by this time, and my mother was sitting on the steps inside the cellar holding on to the rope and pulling on the door as hard as she could. When my dad got to the cellar, he tried to open the door. The harder my daddy pulled on the door handle on the outside, the harder my mother pulled on the rope on the inside. She thought the wind was about to blow the door open. My parents had a real tug of war, but my daddy finally won. He jerked the door open with such a vengeance that it slammed back and nearly ripped off the hinges. When my dad found out my mother had been holding the door closed, he was very upset. He was not nearly as upset as my mother was when she saw the muddy quilt wrapped around my daddy.

My mother raised chickens to supplement our family food supply. These chickens were free to roam the area around our house during the day. At night, they were put into a wire-enclosed coop to protect them from predators. The chickens generously gave an offering of fresh eggs daily and occasionally made a sacrifice to provide a meal for our family. Along with the hens that provided eggs, there was usually a hen or two setting on a nest to keep their eggs warm so they would hatch into baby chickens. After about three weeks, the eggs hatched and baby chickens emerged from the cracked eggs. Some of the female baby chickens were kept to replace the older hens that were past the egg-laying age. These older hens were usually killed, stewed and used to make chicken and dumplings. When the other baby chickens were about six to eight weeks old, they were just right to be used as fryers. My mother was the one in our family who killed and dressed the chickens. If she needed an older hen to stew or one of the young chickens to fry, she enticed them into the coop by scattering chicken feed inside. When they came into the coop, she closed the chickens in, selected the one she wanted and caught it with a wire hook that my dad made her for this very purpose. Then she took the chicken outside the coop, caught it by the head and swung it round and round in her hand as she held on to the head. Before long, the head separated from the body, and the headless chicken flopped around on the ground for a while. After that, my mother plucked the feathers from the chicken's body and held it over an open flame for a few seconds to singe any remaining feathers. She cut the feet off the chicken and removed its internal organs, saving the gizzard and liver. Then she plunged the chicken up and down in a pot of boiling water. All of this was done outside the house. Finally she took the chicken inside, washed it again and prepared it for cooking. Hens were stewed whole in a large pan of water. The fryers were cut into pieces, salted and peppered, rolled in flour and fried in hot grease. With a family the size of ours, my mother usually fried two chickens at a time. For company on Sunday, she would fry three or more chickens. No matter how many chickens my mother cooked, she always ate the back piece of the chicken. I could not understand why anyone would choose the bony back when there was a platter filled with legs, thighs, breast and other meat-laden pieces. I was grown with children of my own before I fully appreciated my mother's unselfish love for her family.

Gathering eggs was a job I did not like. The roosters knew I was afraid of them so they tried to chase me out of the chicken pen. It usually took several tries for me to successfully maneuver past the roosters and gather the eggs from the hen's nest. Once I reached under a hen to retrieve an egg and felt something cold and slimy. I quickly jerked my hand back and scared the hen. When she jumped off the nest, I saw a big snake in the back of the box. I threw my basket of eggs straight up and ran screaming for the house. My mother told me the snake was a chicken snake and perfectly harmless; however, I was not convinced and still have a fear of snakes to this day.

Barbara and I really got in trouble over the chickens one Sunday afternoon. Oleta Jackson and her three sons, Kenneth, Roy and James, came to our house. The three boys and Barbara and I were outside playing. We had been to Steiner Church that morning, so we decided to play church. Our church service started with us singing a few hymns at the top of our lungs. Then Kenneth preached and probably one or two of us got saved. We knew we should baptize someone, but we did not have anything big enough to baptize one of us. A bright idea occurred to someone in the crowd to baptize some of my mother's baby chickens. Imagine our surprise when the chickens came out of the water totally lifeless! Barbara and I were really glad we had company when our mother found out we killed several of her baby chickens. By the time the company left, our mother was not quite as mad as she was in the beginning.

Milk for our family came from a cow that my mother milked. Milking this cow was a daily battle of wills between the cow and my mother. The cow tried every trick she could think of to keep my mother from getting a bucket of milk. The first thing my mother did was wash the teats. Knowing my mother's feelings regarding cleanliness, she probably gave the teats a good, hard scrubbing. This usually did not go over well with the cow and she kicked at my mother. Then the cow stubbornly refused to move her leg so my mother could reach her bag. After the actual milking started, the cow swished her cocklebur-laden tail and hit my mother in the face. Often when the milk bucket was almost full, the cow gave one last kick and turned the bucket over. My mother was a small person, barely five feet tall, but she was not one to admit defeat of any kind. No matter how long it took, she persevered until she won the milking war.

Besides the fresh milk my mother got from the cow for the family's use, she made cream, buttermilk and butter. After she separated the cream, she churned it in a large, earthenware churn. The top of the churn had a hole in the middle and a long stick protruded through the hole. A dasher that looked something like a potato masher was on the end of the stick that was in the churn. The stick with the dasher on the end was plunged up and down in the churn until butter formed. Turning cream into butter was not a fast process. I remember watching my mother, Bonnie or Ma Cole sitting in a hard, straight-back chair churning the butter for what seemed like hours.

- 6 -

My Playground and Playmates

My childhood playground was a wonderful place with few boundaries. If I got bored playing in the house, I could always go into the store area and amuse myself for hours. The buildings surrounding my home and the Steiner store were also part of my playground and provided limitless opportunities for adventure.

One building near the Steiner store was the blacksmith shop run by my grandfather, Pa Cole. When my grandfather comes to my mind, I think about how he dressed. He wore a heavy, long sleeved, cotton shirt in the summer and the winter. The neck of the shirt was buttoned all the way to the top. Suspenders supported his dark-colored, cotton trousers. I never remember him wearing a belt, just suspenders. He carried a walking stick in his hand more to use against animals than for actual support. Heavy, dark frames held the thick lens of his glasses. He always wore a hat, straw in the summer and felt in the winter, on his head. My memories of Pa are mostly from Steiner, as he died soon after we moved to Meridian.

Pa spent a lot of his time in the blacksmith shop repairing wagon parts, sharpening plows and tools, making horseshoes and performing other blacksmith jobs for the folks around Steiner. The blacksmith shop contained an assortment of metal parts and objects waiting for Pa's magical touch. There was an open forge at the back of the blacksmith shop that always had an extremely hot fire burning in it. It was amazing to me how my grandfather could take a piece of metal, heat it until it was fiery red and then hammer it into the shape he wanted it to be. He had a large, steel anvil that he used for shaping metal objects. The anvil later belonged to my daddy, and before he died, he gave it to my husband, James. James has this anvil in his shop and would not part with it. When I see the anvil, I am reminded of the blacksmith shop at Steiner and how I liked to watch my grandfather at work. Even though I enjoyed spending time in the blacksmith shop, my mother did not like for me to play there. She was afraid I might get hurt or burned, and she *knew* I would get very dirty.

A gristmill joined one side of the blacksmith shop. People brought corn to the gristmill and had it ground into meal. At times, they had the corn ground coarsely and mixed with other grains for chicken feed. Ready mixed feed was sometimes available in the feedstore. This feed came in sacks that later would be used to make someone a dress.

The gristmill area frightened me because of all the conveyor belts, motors and loud noise. I did not spend much time in the gristmill, but I loved playing in the room where sacks of feed were stored. It was easy to imagine the colorful sacks becoming a dress for me to wear. If other children were there to play with me, we would move the sacks around and make forts and have imaginary battles. Unfortunately, we were not the only ones who found the feed store an inviting place. On occasion, our playtime ended abruptly when large mice ran out from under the sacks of feed as we moved them around.

Attached to the blacksmith shop on the opposite side from the gristmill was my daddy's automobile garage. This is the area where my dad worked on cars for people in the Steiner area. My daddy was a good mechanic and had mastered car engines of that time. It amazed me how he could take a motor apart, scatter pieces everywhere, and later, put the motor back together and it would actually run.

My dad's garage was another place my mother did not want Barbara and me to play because everything there was greasy. At times, we could not resist playing there, but it was not easy to hide this from our mother. One day, Barbara and I were running around playing by the garage. My dad had changed the oil in someone's vehicle and the open pan containing the old oil sat on the ground. Barbara ran by the pan, lost her balance and fell into the oil. When I saw what happened and how funny she looked with oil all over her, I started laughing. This made Barbara mad and she jumped up, started chasing me and left a trail of oil behind her. Of course I ran for the house, but she caught me before I got there and tackled me. We rolled around in the dirt and oil until both of us were covered. When we got to the house, it did not take long for our mother to figure out where we had been playing.

Before I started school, my grandparents, Ma and Pa Cole, lived in an apartment that joined the back of the blacksmith shop. Since this was just a short distance from our house, I spent a lot of time there. Ma was very patient with me, oftentimes allowing me to help her cook or assist with the household chores. One chore I especially liked was sweeping. To cut down on dust during sweeping, Ma tore rag strips, wet them and put them all around the room before she swept. My job was to tear the rags into strips, wet them and distribute them around the room. Ma would then sweep, ending at the door where she swept everything outside.

Ma had a pillow on her bed that spoke volumes about her. This was a pillow that Ma made and embroidered the words, "In God We Thrust" on the front. After I started to school, I saw that Ma had misspelled a word on the pillow. I wanted to tell her it should be "Trust," and not "Thrust," but I never did. As I got older, I realized it did not matter that she misspelled the word. The meaning was there for her, and the pillow summed up her attitude about life. She totally trusted God in all that she did.

Even though my grandmother was a strong Christian with a very gentle spirit, she had a tooth missing that got knocked out in a fight. This was a fight that she accidentally got into. Once when my daddy and his brother, Lois, were younger, they had a disagreement. The disagreement soon escalated into a full-fledged fistfight. Ma decided it was time to stop her sons from fighting before one of them got hurt. Just as she stepped between the two boys to stop the fight, one of them swung their fist at the other one. The fist hit Ma squarely in the mouth and knocked a tooth out. She never knew which boy's fist hit her. According to my dad, it was his brother, Lois, who hit Ma. According to Uncle Lois, my dad was the one who landed the blow to Ma's mouth. Regardless of who hit her, we enjoyed teasing Ma about how she got her tooth knocked out in a fistfight.

Ma was a very good cook. I loved her chicken and dumplings and hunked potatoes. My mother made good chicken and dumplings, but they were not as good as the ones Ma made. I guess she had more practice than my mother. The hunked potatoes were really just potato soup, but we never called them that. When I was little, I had earache often. Anytime Ma heard I was not feeling well, she would make me some hunked potatoes. It never failed that my ear felt better after a warm bowl of Ma's hunked potatoes.

In January 1945 my dad bought a small house and three acres of land from J.E. Vinson. This house was up the road toward Kopperl about half a mile from the Steiner store. Ma and Pa moved into this house and sometimes I stayed overnight with them. Although I was still very close to my home, spending the night away was a special adventure for me. Ma and Pa's neighbors at first were Eula Payne and her daughters, Maxine and Pauline. After Eula and her daughters moved, Tracy, Loretta and Sherry Brown occupied the house next door to Ma and Pa. Sherry and her parents lived on the Burleson/Johns' farm down the road from the Steiner store until 1946. They moved next door to Ma and Pa when they left the Burleson/Johns' farm. This was a perfect arrangement for me, as Sherry and I were best friends. Since my parents were busy making a living, they had little time to entertain me. Bonnie was almost ten years older and really more like a mother to me than a playmate. Barbara started school two years before I did and I had no one to play with at home. After Barbara started to school, I enjoyed spending the night with Ma and Pa even more so Sherry and I could play together. Sherry started school a year after me and, in our early days at Steiner, the two of us were inseparable. As a result of both of us being double promoted, and perhaps fate, the two of us ended up in the same grade later in our school careers. Sherry and I spent our high school years together, and both graduated from Meridian High School in 1958.

Sherry and I played together at Sherry's house, at Ma and Pa's house next door, at my house or the area around the Steiner store. Once, Sherry and I were playing at Sherry's house and my head kept itching. Sherry's mother, Loretta, saw me scratching my head and examined it to see what was wrong. She found a large tick burrowed on the left side of my head. Loretta pulled the tick off my head, and after I went home, I forgot all about it. A few days later I noticed that the spot where the tick had been was really sore. My mother looked at the place and found the head of the tick embedded in my head. She saturated the spot with alcohol and finally got the tick-head out. In a few weeks, the hair on that spot fell out. My head looked so funny with a bald spot about the size of a silver dollar on one side. By this time, I no longer had the naturally curly hair that I had when I was little. My hair was now totally straight and cut short. When the hair came back on the bald spot, it was one big curl. I looked even funnier then with a head full of straight hair except the one curly spot.

Sherry and I had several favorite places we liked to play. One of these was in Ma and Pa's yard under a chinaberry tree. We built a playhouse under this tree and spent many hours playing there. First we gathered all the rocks we could find. Then we used the rocks to outline the outside walls and rooms of our playhouse. Sherry and I took turns being the mother and the daddy; our dolls were our children.

One day Sherry and I were playing in our playhouse under the chinaberry tree. Ma made some fried green grape pies and gave each of us one. If you have never eaten a fried green grape pie you do not know what you have missed. Sherry and I could hardly wait to eat our pies, but they were fresh out of the pan and too hot to eat. We left them on a plate in our playhouse to cool while we went in the house for a minute. When we came back outside, Ma and Pa's dog had eaten our pies. If we could have caught that dog, it would have been in serious trouble.

At a very young age, Sherry and I were entrepreneurs, as we owned and operated a small business in the pasture behind the Steiner store. The two of us were partners in a first-class stick horse ranch. We made these stick horses from old broom and mop handles. The reins were fashioned with a piece of string put through a hole in one end of the stick and knotted together on the ends. After we established our stick horse ranch, our attention turned to how we, as owners of a respectable horse ranch, should dress. For this we looked to our heroes, Roy Rogers and Gene Autry. We wore wide-brimmed cowboy hats and tied handkerchiefs around our necks. Of course, we always had our cap pistols loaded and strapped to our waist in case horse thieves showed up. Our bare feet stayed busy corralling wild horses on our ranch under a tree in the pasture.

If Sherry and I were not managing our stick horse ranch or playing at Ma and Pa's or Sherry's house, she, Barbara and I played together at our house. One place the three of us enjoyed was a play area on top of the icehouse in our kitchen. According to my brother, Mearl, my daddy bought an old building at Brazos Point, dismantled it and used the lumber to build partitions and different rooms in our house. One such room was the icehouse located in our kitchen. The icehouse was a dark, insulated room, probably no larger than ten feet square, where ice was stored. Sheets of tin nailed inside thick, wooden walls helped insulate the room and keep the ice from melting.

All the ceilings in our house were high except for the icehouse ceiling. When my dad built the icehouse inside our kitchen, the top of it was several feet lower than the main ceiling of the kitchen. This created a space between the top of the icehouse and the kitchen ceiling. My dad made a wooden ladder and attached it to the side of the icehouse so we could climb to the top. This was our playhouse area, and we spent many hours playing there in the hot summer months. The ice in the icehouse cooled our playhouse. With no air conditioning in the house, the playhouse on top of the icehouse was probably the coolest area in the house.

At first my dad and Mearl drove to the ice plant in Walnut Springs and bought large, scored blocks of ice. These blocks weighed one hundred to three hundred pounds. When the plant in Walnut Springs closed, my dad bought ice in Meridian. At the ice plant, my daddy backed up to the loading area, and an employee guided the big blocks of ice down a tin chute into the back of my dad's pickup. Then my dad and Mearl covered the ice with tarpaulins and quickly drove back to the Steiner store before it melted. They divided the large blocks into fifty-pound blocks and stored them in the icehouse in our kitchen. People in the Steiner community came to the store and purchased ice for their iceboxes. For really special occasions, they purchased ice to make homemade ice cream. When they came to buy ice, they backed up to the side porch outside our kitchen. From the porch, a door led directly into the kitchen where the icehouse was located. Many times when people came to buy ice, my dad was working on someone's car in his shop. Since the shop was on the other side of the store building, he would not be aware there was an ice customer. My mother was often working in the kitchen, and would get the ice out of the icehouse and load it into the customer's vehicle. She used ice tongs to grasp the block of ice and drag it out of the icehouse onto the side porch. This porch was several feet off the ground.

One day my mother was dragging a large block of ice with the ice tongs to a customer's vehicle. As she backed across the porch dragging the ice, she somehow misjudged where she was and fell off the porch. She and the block of ice took a pretty good tumble off the high porch. Bonnie was watching all this happen, and as soon as she saw that our mother was okay, she started laughing.

My mother pulled herself up to her full five feet, looked at Bonnie and said, "I'll declare, Bonnie, if I would have broken my neck, I guess you still would have laughed!"

Barbara and I were always sending off box tops and other things in order to receive prizes. Once, we saw an advertisement for a free animal picture book. Since the book was something we really did want, and since it was free we sent away for it. The book came and was just as wonderful as advertised. We spent many hours looking at the pictures of animals we had never seen before in our life. Before too long, we began to receive letters from the company saying we owed them money for the book. These threatening letters continued for weeks. We were afraid to tell our parents because we thought we would be in trouble. Barbara and I felt sure someone was going to come get us and put us in jail. With that experience, we learned that nothing in life is really free. We also found out that you better read the fine print before you order something.

During my growing up years, playtime was uncomplicated. If I did not have anyone to play with, I amused myself by reading a book, playing with my dolls, kicking a can or any number of things. By today's standard, children would be bored living in the world I lived in; however, I would not trade my childhood for theirs. Life was so different in the days before terrorists' attacks and school shootings. Today's young generation has many tribulations that rob them of the trouble-free years of their childhood. There are moments when I wish I could turn back the hands of the clock to those carefree, timeless days of yesteryear, but I have a feeling if I did, some of the simple pleasures of my childhood years would not be there.

- 7 -

School Days

Verna Pallmeyer and her husband, W.C. Pallmeyer, got married in 1919 and moved to the Steiner area at that time. According to Mrs. Pallmeyer, at least four schools were in the Steiner vicinity during the years, and she taught at all four. Some of these schools dated from the early 1900's. Mrs. Pallmeyer said the schools sometimes had one teacher, sometimes two. By the 1930's all of the schools had ceased to function.

The first school at Steiner was a one-room schoolhouse. Later a two-story building was built. The lower floor was the school and the upper story was a lodge hall. After this the school was a two-room building. During the week the building was used for school, and on the weekend, the Church of Christ met there for their services. Some of the teachers at Steiner schools were Carl Rose, Otto Shelley, Willie Belle Vinson, Dessie Raines, Mattie Lou Lane and Verna Pallmeyer. The Steiner School consolidated with Kopperl in the 1930's.

New Home School was in the Allen Bend area below Steiner. The New Home School consolidated with Kopperl before Steiner School did.

Another school was in the Cedron area. The school used the building during the week and Cedron Baptist Church met there on Sunday.

The fourth school was at Bodine, not far from where Lakeside Village is now. The H.L. Downey family later used this building for a hay barn.

By the time my sister, Bonnie, started school in 1937, the school at Steiner had consolidated with Kopperl School. Bonnie, Mearl, Barbara and I all began our school careers at Kopperl, but Bonnie was the only one who graduated from Kopperl High School.

I was almost five years old when my sister Barbara started to school in September 1945. On her first day of school, I was very distraught. I really do not know why, as Barbara and I fought unceasingly. It seems that I would have been happy to see her go to school. Up to this point, anything Barbara did I was allowed to do; therefore, I felt sure

I was going to school that year also. When the bus stopped in front of the Steiner store, Barbara got on. I was very upset when my parents would not let me join her. As the bus and Barbara left without me, I shot the back window out with my slingshot. Later, my dad owned part of that bus. It was a small part, but a window is a window.

I outsmarted them though. The way I figured it, they might not let me go to school, but they could not stop me from learning. Every day when Barbara got home from school I talked her into being my teacher. Barbara called out her spelling words and I learned them along with her. She made up arithmetic problems for me to work, and taught me from her reader. I knew all about Dick, Jane, Sally and Spot long before I started to school. I still have a little schoolbook dated September 1, 1945 with the contract price of fifty-four cents written in the back of the book. I had mastered this book and most of the first grade work before I started to school.

In September 1947, a few days shy of my seventh birthday, my time to start school finally came. Barbara was in third grade this year and Bonnie was a senior. My brother, Mearl, was no longer in school. Mearl was hard of hearing, and in those days, there were no special education classes for the hearing-impaired. Mearl was forced to attend regular school classes and every day was a struggle for him. Finally when he was in the fifth grade, my parents allowed him to quit school.

I will never forget the day I started first grade. I stood in front of the store in my feed sack dress and new shoes waiting for the bus to come. My Big Chief writing tablet, large pencil and wooden ruler were clutched firmly in my hands. By this season of my life, I had made the important discovery that crime did not pay. My early rebellious years of shooting school bus windows with my slingshot were forever behind me. Today, the bus would welcome me as a passenger. Finally the big, yellow bus came and I was off to begin my school career. I remember looking back and waving at my mother and daddy as the bus drove off. I also remember that the world seemed so big as I looked out the window of that bus on the seven-mile drive to Kopperl. Little did I know, as I began my journey of searching for knowledge, my world would never be the same.

My first grade classroom was in a small, one-story, frame structure set apart from the other buildings on the Kopperl campus. Inside, blackboards lined the front wall of the lone room. In the following months, I became good friends with those blackboards as I stood before the class and worked arithmetic problems or printed spelling words.

The first and second grades were in the same room. Mrs. Alta Day taught both classes. On my first day of school, Mrs. Day instructed us to call her "Miss Alta." Miss Alta's husband, Truett Day, was Superintendent of Kopperl schools.

The first lesson I learned in school had to do with talking. Miss Alta said there were certain times she wanted us to talk and certain times she did not. This was a difficult thing for me to comprehend because I liked to talk. I did not understand why it mattered when you talked if you had something you really wanted to say. One day when I was talking to my friends, I discovered if Miss Alta told you something you better listen. I learned she meant business and was not one to fool with. From that day forward, Miss Alta and I had a perfect understanding of who was boss.

Miss Alta taught me other valuable lessons. I learned it was a very bad thing to take something that belonged to someone else. Not long after I started first grade, Miss Alta told the two classes someone had taken another person's lunch money. She said if we had taken this money we should give it back. Miss Alta marched everyone outside and lined us up. She told each first and second grade student to go into the school house one at a time, and if we had taken the money we should put it in her desk drawer. If we had not taken the money we were to go in, stay a few minutes and come out without opening the drawer. Miss Alta said no one would ever know who took the money and no one would get in trouble. She also said if the money was not put back, we would not go to lunch at our regular period. I knew I did not take the money, but I was traumatized by the thought of missing lunch. I had my money in my pocket and thought about putting it in the drawer so we could go to lunch on time. Then I remembered if I did that, I would not have money to pay for my lunch. When my time came, I went into the schoolhouse, stayed for just a little while and came out. Every first and second grader had their turn, and then Miss Alta went in and looked in the drawer. When she came out, she had a big smile on her face. After we got back in the classroom Miss Alta said she was very proud that the person who took the money was brave enough to put it back. She said she hoped they learned a lesson they would never forget. I do not know if they learned a lesson or not but I know I did. I have never forgotten this lesson.

Since the first and second grades were in the same room, Miss Alta divided her time between the two classes. During the first part of the morning, Miss Alta worked with the first grade students. Then she assigned us some arithmetic problems or spelling words to study. While we studied, Miss Alta taught the second grade class. This fascinated me. You remember my sister, Barbara, was my teacher long before I started school. When I started first grade, I was *really smart*. Well, I thought I was anyway. I could read the first grade reader and work the arithmetic problems with my eyes closed. Barbara had taught me the spelling words. Miss Alta said study hall was one of those times you did not talk. I had to keep busy and quiet, so I listened to Miss Alta teaching the second graders. I breezed through first grade, and by midterm of the second grade, Miss Alta saw she had a problem with me. To solve this problem, Miss Alta decided I should be promoted to third grade immediately. My report card said Miss Alta promoted me at midterm because of my age and I.Q. Despite what the report card said, I have always suspected Miss Alta wanted to move me through those first two grades as quickly as possible. At any rate, those B's in deportment/conduct did not hold me back like my parents said they would.

The Halloween carnival was a big production at Kopperl School. The carnival and crowning of the queens and kings occurred on the Friday night before October 31. If the weather allowed, the carnival was held outside on the school grounds. Each grade sponsored a booth, sold chances on something and sold baked items and other things to make money for their representatives. The Halloween carnival money was donated to the school

When I was in second grade and Barbara was in fourth, we were selected as Halloween duchesses by our classes. My escort was Ronnie Carlisle. Barbara's escort was Louis Robinson. Barbara and I knew the queen for grades one through eight would be the one who raised the most money. Of course we wanted this coveted honor, but we knew both of us could not win. My daddy built a gasoline-powered car big enough to carry one person. On the night of the carnival we sold tickets for a ride in this car. Our booth was the most popular attraction at the carnival. School kids lined up to purchase a ride around the schoolyard in the cute little car. Since Barbara and I had to split the money between us, neither of us made enough money to win the queen's race. My best friend, Sherry Brown, was crowned Grammar School Queen.

I bought a chance to win twenty-five baby chickens and an incubator at the Halloween carnival that same year. Imagine how thrilled I was when I won those chickens. My mother was happy also. She raised the chickens and when they were grown, made plans to kill some for a meal of fried chicken. I was very upset, but my mother explained to me they were roosters and intended to be used for food. That was okay with me because I certainly did not want more roosters that would chase me from the chicken pen.

May Day was another celebration at Kopperl School. For several weeks before the festivity, we all practiced for the big event. A day or two before the program, everyone pitched in to clean up the schoolyard. On a warm May evening near the end of the school year, parents and children came to the school. Crepe paper streamers of all colors hung from the flagpole. We took our places, dressed in our Sunday best, and grabbed hold of our streamer. As the music played we marched around the flagpole, weaving over and under the next person, until the traditional winding of the Maypole was complete. This was a beautiful ceremony and one I have never forgotten.

I had no problems with first grade and the first half of second grade; however, no one prepared me for third grade. When I was promoted in the middle of the year, I went from mid-semester of second grade to the second semester of third grade overnight. Whereas printing was acceptable in first and second grades, I now had to complete my assignments in cursive writing. The stories in my reader were no longer about Dick, Jane, Sally and Spot. The third grade reader contained long, unfamiliar words that were hard to comprehend. Suddenly arithmetic was extremely difficult, as I was not prepared for multiplication tables and long division. My security blanket was pulled from underneath me. The sheltered environment of the small, one-room schoolhouse had vanished. I had to find my way around in a two-story structure that housed grades three through eight. The building intimidated me because everything was foreign. I have good memories of my first and second grades; however, I remember very little of the second semester I spent in third grade at Kopperl. At the end of the first six-weeks of my fourth grade year, my family moved to Meridian. I attended the remainder of the fourth grade as well as all grades through the twelfth at Meridian.

- 8 -

Fun and Entertainment

People at Steiner relied on their imaginations and simple, traditional games for entertainment. Montgomery Wards and Sears Roebuck catalogues were good sources of amusement for children. These catalogues had several functions. First, they were dream books. We looked at every page and fantasized how we might someday have clothes and shoes like those in the catalogues. Occasionally our parents ordered something from one of the books. We also cut homemade paper dolls and their clothes from the catalogues and spent hours playing with them. Of course the last stop was the outhouse. Even there we flipped through the pages while we waited for Mother Nature to do her thing.

If I were by myself, I read a book, played with my dolls, played jacks or looked through the stereoscope at the double-view picture cards. On occasion I might go outside and play on the tree swing my daddy built from a board and rope. My favorite times were when company came to visit my parents and brought their children. Odell, Lenore, Charles, Anthony and Annalee Steen came to visit often, as did Lee, Vera, Billy, Barbara June and Peggy McCurdy. Barbara and I had so much fun playing with the children outside while our parents visited inside. We played hide-and-seek, red rover, freeze tag, red light-green light, London Bridges, Mother May I and Simon Says until darkness overtook us. Then we caught lightning bugs, put them in empty jelly jars and watched them glow as they flashed in the dark. Finally our bare feet took us inside for cold soda water and maybe a bar of candy.

Once my daddy's brother, Uncle Lois, and his family were at our house. Joy, Jo Ann, Janet, Bonnie, Mearl, Barbara and I were all outside playing and found a dead bird. One of us came up with the idea that we should have a funeral for the bird. We all had our part in the funeral. Joy, being the oldest, appointed herself the undertaker and told the rest of us what to do. Mearl dug the grave and Barbara and I found a small box for the casket.

Bonnie and Jo Ann sang a song. Apparently Janet was the designated crier because she started crying and we could not get her to stop. We all told her it was just a bird and that it was already dead before we found it, but she kept crying. Eventually the grown-ups came out of the house and wanted to know who hurt Janet. After we explained the story to them, they tried to get Janet to stop crying. Even with the grown-ups talking to Janet, it was a long time before she stopped crying.

Sunday was the Lord's Day and my parents did not work on that day. The store, garage, blacksmith shop, everything, was closed on Sunday. After we ate Sunday dinner we had free time, so Sunday afternoons were fun times at Steiner. Since Steiner store was the central gathering place for the community, kinfolks or neighbors often stopped by for a visit during the afternoon. One thing everybody liked to do was play croquet. The croquet court was across the road from the Steiner store on the other side of the railroad tracks. Just recently, Kid Rich mentioned that Mace Brooks helped my dad build the croquet court. I do not remember when the croquet court was built, nor do I remember a time when it was not there. My dad, Mace Brooks and perhaps others hauled sand from the creek and used this sand to level the ground for the croquet court. My dad and Pa Cole built heavy-duty wickets for the court. When neighbors or kinfolks came to visit, we played game after game of croquet. There was an area for horseshoes and washers at one end of the croquet court. People alternated from croquet to games of horseshoes or washers. Younger boys sometimes shot marbles while the girls played with their dolls or jumped rope.

Since the railroad track was near the croquet ground, we often placed a penny on the track. After we put the penny down, we lowered our ear to the cold, steel track to feel for vibrations from an approaching train. If we heard a long, far-away whistle of a train we ran back from the railroad track. After the train passed, everyone scrambled to look for the penny. The child who found the penny usually squealed with delight. We all gathered around to look at the long, squashed coin void of any imprint.

Many Sunday afternoons in the summertime the women went to our house and made freezers of ice cream. If peaches were in season, the ice cream might be fresh peach; otherwise, vanilla or banana was the flavor of the day. After games of croquet, horseshoes or washers in the hot sun, nothing tasted better than homemade ice cream and cookies or cake that one of the ladies brought. The adults sat on the porch or under a shade tree to eat and visit. The children stopped only long enough to grab a bowl of ice cream and some cake before they were off to play again.

If a car passed by, we all waved at the people in the car. There were few strangers at Steiner, but it did not matter whether we knew someone or not, we still waved. It was just the country way of doing things. Everybody was your neighbor and friend. No one locked their doors at night or when they went somewhere. Come to think of it, we probably did not even have locks on our doors.

Another favorite thing to do in the summertime was go swimming in Steele Creek. The best swimming hole near our house was just below Steiner Church where you crossed Steele Creek to go to the Townley's house. Sometimes families gathered at this swimming hole on the Fourth of July for a picnic and afternoon of swimming and relaxation. The running water was clean and clear, especially on the rocks in the shallow part of the creek bed. There were springs in the bank of the creek that ran cool water even on the hottest days of summer.

Thinking about the springs and cool water of Steele Creek reminds me of how my aunt and Uncle, Velma and C.W. Potts, loved to come to Steiner and camp out near Steele Creek. Aunt Velma was my mother's sister, and she and "Potts," as we called her husband, lived in Ft. Worth and came to Steiner occasionally for a camping trip. On the way to their campsite, Aunt Velma and Potts stopped at the Steiner store and bought a big block of ice and invited us to come eat with them that evening. I remember two things about the meals we ate with them. The first is sliced bologna. Aunt Velma and Potts always brought a large, paper-wrapped package of fresh sliced bologna with them from Ft. Worth. I thought Aunt Velma and Potts surely had to be rich—after all they lived in the city and could afford things like bologna. You have to know that Steiner folks were not acquainted with gourmet food like sliced bologna. With no electricity, there was no way to keep lunch meat. The second thing I remember about eating with Aunt Velma and Potts is their refrigerator. Potts had built this refrigerator before we got to where they were camping. First, he dug a hole in the ground. Then he put the food items that needed to be kept cool in a tow sack and put this sack into the hole. The block of ice that he bought at the Steiner store was put on top of the tow sack, and all of this was covered with a thin layer of dirt. This "refrigerator" kept their food cool all during their camping trip.

People at Steiner were always looking for ways to pass the time of day. Once, Tracy Brown and my daddy provided some scary entertainment for the community. An old churn, some leather, baling wire and rawhide made an interesting device. Tracy and my dad cut two slits in a piece of leather and ran a strip of rawhide through the slits. Then they stretched the leather across the top of the churn and secured it with the baling wire. When they pulled the rawhide strip back and forth through the slits in the leather, the result was a loud, eerie, animal-like sound. They named their invention "the swacker." The men decided it would be funny to try the swacker at night. They secretly got together one night and pulled the rawhide strip through the leather several times. Those who heard the sound thought some dangerous creature was lurking in the shadows. By the next day, the story had circulated throughout the Steiner community and there was major panic. People envisioned some wild animal roaming the area around Steiner. Fear intensified each time the story was repeated. Finally

Tracy and my dad laughingly told everyone about the swacker. They were the only ones in the community who saw the humor in the situation.

One September Sunday happened to be my eighth birthday. After we ate dinner, some friends and kinfolks stopped by to visit and play croquet. I did not notice anything different about this Sunday afternoon. As usual, I played with the other children and had a good time. At one point the ladies went across the road to our house and made ice cream. Again, this was nothing out of the ordinary as they did this most summer Sunday afternoons. When we all went to the house for ice cream, everyone hollered, "Happy Birthday!" Bonnie brought a birthday cake out of the house and I got a few gifts. The only gift I remember was a white, milk glass covered chicken. I played with this chicken for years until I finally broke the bottom. Perhaps my love for this gift explains why I now have an antique covered-chicken collection.

My daddy's sister and brother-in law, Eunita and Uncle Allen Shafer, and their children, Gloria and Maurice, lived in the Steiner area for a while. Maurice was known as "Sonny" to all of us. Once when they were at our house, Gloria told a story about how she killed a possum a few days before.

Sonny argued with her and said he was the one who killed the possum. Before long, Gloria and Sonny were in a heated argument over who killed the possum. Finally their mother told the real possum story. According to Eunita, Gloria was outside playing and saw a possum. She hit the possum with a stick, it fell to the ground and lay motionless, pretending to be dead. Gloria thought she killed it. Later Sonny came along and found the same possum that was alive and well. He hit it with a stick and thought he killed it because it again pretended to be dead. Both of them told Eunita about killing the possum and she went outside and there was no dead possum. Neither Gloria nor Sonny wanted to admit that the animal was just "playing possum" because they both wanted to claim the honor of killing the possum.

When young couples got married in the Steiner community, they usually went to a preacher's house for the ceremony. According to Loretta Brown, Sherry's mother, newly married Steiner couples rarely went anywhere for their honeymoon. After the wedding, if they were lucky enough to have a house of their own, they went to this house. More often they did not have a house to go to and spent their wedding night with one of their parents. Since

Steiner was such a close-knit community, word usually got around about the wedding. Steiner folks would go to the newlywed's house and serenade them with a shivaree. They stood outside the house, sang, beat on pots and pans and made noise any way they could. Eventually the young couple opened the door and the group congratulated them on their marriage. Sometimes they were invited into the house to share a piece of wedding cake with the bride and groom.

As summer came to a close, it became more difficult to find things to occupy our time. In the fall when pecans started falling, we went to the Wallace place and picked up sacks full of pecans. We kept some of these for our use and, depending on the crop each year, occasionally sold some. On long winter evenings, we gathered around the wood stove and shelled pecans. My daddy cut the ends and sides off the pecans with his pocketknife and we finished shelling them. Before the evening was over we had a large pan of freshly shelled pecans ready for Christmas baking.

When Bonnie was in high school, she often had girlfriends who spent the night with her. Two of Bonnie's close friends were Nelda Ruth Newsome and Mary Lou Downey. Barbara and I enjoyed it when Nelda Ruth or Mary Lou spent the night at our house. Most likely Bonnie did not like us hanging around them because we were probably pests. Bonnie played basketball and on game days, Nelda came home with Bonnie after school. If the game was a home game, my parents, Bonnie, Nelda, Mearl, Barbara and I went to Kopperl for the game. If the game was an out of town game, just Bonnie and Nelda drove to Kopperl, caught the bus and went to the game. After all of the basketball games, Nelda came back to our house with Bonnie and spent the night.

Bonnie, Mearl, Barbara and I played a lot of card games during long, winter evenings. Two of our favorite games were Flinch and Canasta. Many times we popped popcorn on the old wood stove, made hot chocolate and homemade candy. Saturday nights, we listened to "Fibber McGee and Molly," and "Amos and Andy" on our big, battery-powered radio.

The area around the Steiner store was transformed into a beautiful, winter wonderland when it snowed. We put on the warmest clothes we had and went outside to play in the snow. If there was enough snow, we made a snowman, complete with button eyes, an old hat and corncob pipe.

Small balls of snow were wonderful weapons for a snowball fight. We played in the snow until we were too cold to stay outside any longer, and then rushed into the house and warmed by the old wood stove.

Snow ice cream was a treat we often made when it snowed. To make this ice cream, we hunted until we found clean snow. Usually this was on a low roof or in a snowdrift somewhere. We scooped the snow into a large bowl, took it back to the house and added sugar, vanilla flavoring and milk. This made delicious snow ice cream.

Christmas was a special time at our house. We celebrated Christmas as Jesus' birthday as well as the traditional way that children love. In early December we went to the pasture behind our house, selected the most beautiful tree we could find and took the tree back to our house. My daddy nailed boards to the bottom of the tree so it would stand up. Then we took it inside the house and decorated it. Our only store-bought decorations were a few strands of lights and some silver tinsel icicles. The lights were the kind with large bulbs; if one of the bulbs burned out, the entire string quit working. Usually before the Christmas season ended, several bulbs burned out and were replaced. Sometimes we used all our replacement bulbs and the lights ceased to burn. Our other Christmas tree decorations were homemade. We popped popcorn, ate some and used a needle and thread to make long strings of popcorn. We made colorful chains with construction paper and paste. Each year after Christmas, we carefully removed the lights and silver icicles from the tree and saved them for the next year.

During the Christmas season, our living room resembled a magical kingdom. The brightly colored decorations on the Christmas tree, the lingering smell of wood burning in the wood stove together with the pervasive scent of the cedar Christmas tree contributed to the feeling of enchantment. If I concentrate for a minute, this sensation returns to me even today.

I do not remember many presents—there probably were not many—but we always thought Santa brought so much. One present I do remember is a shiny red bicycle Santa left for Barbara and me together. Between the two of us, we rode that bicycle many miles. Once when we had company, someone was on the bicycle and Barbara was riding on the back. Her bare foot got caught in the bicycle chain and her heel was cut badly. We all learned a lesson that day about riding double on the bicycle.

My mother always made an old-fashioned fruitcake at Christmas. She baked the cake soon after Thanksgiving in a heavy, rectangular pan lined with waxed paper. After the cake cooled, she wrapped it in a clean cup towel and stored it in a box under the bed until Christmas. Old-fashioned fruitcakes were traditionally soaked in some kind of alcoholic beverage to keep them moist. My mother, the Baptist preacher's wife, did not follow this tradition, but her fruitcakes were always moist and delicious.

Brother W.L. Cass was one of the pastors of Steiner Baptist Church in the early 1940's. His wife, Dorothy, gave my mother a recipe for divinity candy. This was my daddy's favorite candy, so my mother always made a batch or two at Christmas. Since we did not have an electric mixer, it took several people to beat the candy by hand. Often, Lenora Steen came to help make this divinity. Bonnie would beat awhile, and then my mother, Ma Cole and Lenore would all take their turns beating the candy. Barbara and I helped also—we were the official tasters. Yum, that slightly warm divinity candy loaded with freshly shelled pecans tasted so good.

Barbara and I could hardly wait for Christmas Day to come. Of course, we were up early to see what Santa brought us. My mother was also up early preparing food for the noon meal. Christmas dinner was quite a production in the Cole household. My mother made chicken or duck dressing, mashed potatoes and giblet gravy, for starters. Candied sweet potatoes, homemade cranberry sauce, corn, green beans and boogered eggs were usually on the Christmas menu. In case you do not know what boogered eggs are, let me explain. Since my grandparents, Ma and Pa Cole, lived near us, they were always at our house for holiday meals. My grandmother was a very devout Christian who greatly influenced my life. She refused to say any word she considered even slightly sinful. One such word that fit this category as far as my grandmother was concerned was the word "devil." When deviled eggs were served at our house, Ma called them "boogered eggs." Ma has been gone for many years now. Today, almost sixty years since my childhood days at Steiner, deviled eggs are still known as "boogered eggs" to my children, grandchildren and great-grandchildren.

Following my mother's wonderful Christmas meal, we had several dessert choices. Besides homemade candy and fruitcake, other Christmas desserts were pies—lots of pies. My mother made mince meat, apple, peach, chocolate, coconut, pecan and other pies for Christmas. Sometimes she made as many as thirty pies, all with homemade crust. She started baking pies several days before Christmas. She baked two or three pies at a time and let them cool. Then she slid them from the pan onto a piece of waxed paper and stacked them on top of each other. She kept this up until she was satisfied she had enough pies. Before Christmas was over, the pies were all eaten, as we had lots of company during the holidays.

- 9 -

Remember the Sabbath Day

Fowler Baptist Church was organized as a Southern Baptist Church in 1891. Brother E.D. Wallace was the first pastor and was still pastor in 1895 when the membership was forty-six. In the beginning, there was no church building, so services were held in homes or in a building in town.

Joseph Madison Yates donated a parcel of land to Fowler Baptist Church in 1906. This land was near the railroad tracks and Steele Creek. Fowler citizens helped build a church building on this land. In 1907 the church burned, but citizens rebuilt the building in 1908 at the original location.

Fowler Baptist Church was later renamed Steiner Baptist Church. A brush arbor was built a short distance below the church, near Steele Creek, in the summer of 1928. It was during the construction of this arbor that James M. Wallace suffered a fatal fall.

During the 1940's Cedron Baptist Church united with Steiner Baptist Church. In 1950 the Steiner Baptist Church building built in 1908 was moved to a parcel of land donated by Buddy Nitcholas in the Poeville area. This move was necessary due to the construction of Lake Whitney Dam. The original site of Steiner Baptist Church is now under the waters of Lake Whitney.

According to Steiner Baptist Church records, my mother and daddy were both baptized in Steele Creek on August 12, 1925 by the pastor, Brother Billy Greer. Brother Greer also married my parents on December 24, 1929. Soon after my parents were married, my daddy felt that God was calling him to preach, but he did not respond to God's call. In late 1930 my mother was expecting my sister, Bonnie, and my daddy got very sick. When he finally went to the doctor, the doctor determined that my dad had advanced appendicitis. By this time, my dad was extremely sick and had to have an emergency appendectomy. The doctor told my parents my dad might not live. My daddy promised God if He would let him live he would surrender to be a preacher. He did live and after over twenty days in the Whitney hospital, my dad followed through with his promise to God. To prepare himself for the ministry, my dad later attended Southwestern Theological Seminary in Fort Worth. Through the years, my dad preached at Steiner Baptist Church and eventually became the pastor of this church.

Along with preaching, my daddy married some and buried some. My sister, Bonnie, told me the story of one couple my dad married. Odell Steen and Lenore Stephenson asked my dad to marry them. He performed their marriage ceremony in July 1936. He must have done a good job because Odell and Lenore celebrated their fiftieth wedding anniversary in July 1986. When Odell died in September 1998 he and Lenore were still married.

The people who attended Steiner Baptist Church were poor, country farmers struggling to make a living. Although they were strong Christian folks, they had very little money to spare to support a church. As a result, the church could not afford a full-time pastor. Every other Sunday a preacher from the seminary in Fort Worth came to Steiner to preach. Some preachers I remember from the seminary are W.L. Cass, A.D. Caraway, Brother Worley and Brother Lemon. On the Sundays when a seminary preacher did not come to Steiner my daddy preached.

Brother W.L. Cass, or Louis, and his wife, Dorothy, were wonderful Christian people who remained friends with my family for the remainder of their lives. They had two sons, Joe Warren and Don, who were around the age of Barbara and me. Don, like his dad, became a minister in later years. He has held positions in the field of Evangelism in both New Mexico and Texas.

One weekend, Brother Cass and his family spent Saturday night at our house. Following church on Sunday, they went home with church members for lunch. They came back to our house before church that evening. We noticed Brother Cass taking something from his coat pockets and soon saw it was biscuits. Brother Cass told us the story of how the lady passed him the pan of biscuits and he took two. When he bit into one of the biscuits it was hard and tasted very bad so he slipped both biscuits into his coat pocket. Soon the lady noticed he was out of biscuits and passed him the pan again. This time he took only one biscuit, and when no one was looking, slipped it into his coat pocket. Several times more the lady passed the biscuits. Each time, Brother Cass took one and as soon as possible, slipped it into his pocket. All of us really did laugh at him when he was unloading the biscuits from his pockets.

People have told me I had really beautiful, naturally curly hair when I was little. This is hard to imagine because my hair was straight as a board in my first-grade picture. According to family members, Dorothy Cass loved to brush my hair. Dorothy did not have any daughters, and the story goes that she thought I was very pretty and wanted to brush my hair often. Being a typical little child, I was constantly moving and Dorothy had to come up with ways to keep me still. She sang to me, told me Bible stories or let me play with articles in her purse to bribe me into allowing her to brush my hair. Although I did not necessarily like to have my hair brushed, I did love sitting in Dorothy's lap. I can remember wanting to go home with the Cass family.

In later years Dorothy told a funny story that happened to her one Sunday at Steiner. Following the church service, Brother Cass baptized some new Christians in Steele Creek. Dorothy said she had on a new rayon dress and thought she looked unusually pretty that day. A sudden rainstorm came up while Brother Cass was baptizing, and those standing on the creek bank got as wet as the ones in the water. Dorothy said she noticed her dress was getting tighter and tighter. The rain shrank her new rayon dress until it was well above her knees and stretched tight on her body. According to Dorothy, she was very embarrassed. Since she did not have another Sunday dress with her that weekend, she had to borrow a dress from a lady in the church.

Brother A.D. Caraway—Amos—and his wife, Lillian, had four children: Bobby, David, Barbara Ann and Mary Margaret. My sister, Barbara, and I loved playing with the Caraway children. The two boys were older than Barbara and me, Barbara Ann was between us and Mary Margaret was younger.

Mrs. Caraway taught the children's Sunday school class at Steiner Church. She brought a big blackboard and different colors of chalk to church. As she told the Bible story, she drew beautiful chalk drawings to illustrate her words. She drew pictures of Adam and Eve, Noah and the Ark, David and Goliath, Mary and Joseph, Jesus and other Bible characters on the blackboard. These pictures seemed to make the Bible stories come alive. As a young child, her stories and drawings made an impression on me that I have never forgotten.

Brother Worley was a young seminary student who was not married at the time he preached at Steiner. The thing I remember most about Brother Worley is that he was very accident-prone. Brother

Worley, like other preachers who came from the seminary, usually came Saturday afternoon and spent the night in our home. One Sunday morning we were all getting dressed for church when Brother Worley called my dad in a very loud, panicky voice. As it turned out, when Brother Worley zipped his trousers, he broke the zipper. Since this was the only pair of pants he had with him, he was in quite a predicament. My daddy calmed him down as best he could, got his pliers and repaired the zipper.

One Sunday before church my mother made a banana pudding for lunch. She made the pudding my dad's favorite way, with a browned meringue on top. After church my mother put all the food on the table, my daddy asked the blessings and we started eating. Brother Worley was at our house for lunch that day and still had his suit on during the meal. He saw a dish of food on the other side of the table he wanted so he reached out, pointed at the dish and asked my daddy to pass it to him. When he extended his arm, he scraped across the top of the pudding with the sleeve of his coat. With one swift motion he scooped almost all of the meringue into his coat sleeve. Yes, Brother Worley was the preacher everyone remembered for his many accidents.

Brother Lemon was one of the more interesting seminary students who preached at Steiner Church. He was near Brother Worley's age, but unlike Brother Worley, he had a beautiful, young wife. Brother Lemon and his wife came to our house several times on Saturday and spent the night. Our family and the church congregation fell in love with Brother Lemon and his wife. It was not long before Brother Lemon's secret life leaked out. The woman who came with him to Steiner was not his wife. Actually he was married to someone else and they had children together. The woman he brought to Steiner and introduced as his wife was just his girlfriend. The love affair between Brother Lemon, our family and Steiner Baptist Church ended very abruptly.

My family worshipped every Sunday at Steiner Baptist Church. The church was located about two miles from the Steiner store and my home. I am so very fortunate that my grandmother and parents left me such a wonderful Christian heritage to build my life on. It does not surprise me that I have a multitude of cherished memories centering around Steiner Baptist Church.

The church building was a white, frame structure with a high-pitched roof that unmistakably identified it as a rural church. There was nothing impressive about the building on the outside. As I think about the interior, bits and pieces of how it looked come rushing back to me. It is almost as if I am there once again walking through the front door onto the bare plank floors. Strains of "Rock of Ages," "Amazing Grace," and "Beulah Land" saturated the building. Several rows of crude, homemade benches flanked the center aisle. My grandfather, J.W. Cole, helped build these benches. The benches were strictly utilitarian, not built for beauty or comfort. Several copies of the paperback songbook, *Christian Service Songs*, graced each bench. Continuing down the center aisle, the pulpit was straight ahead at the front of the church. One bare light bulb hung over the pulpit. Three or four more bulbs dangled from the ceiling around the room. A weathered, upright piano was to one side near the front of the church. The lone source of heat, an old wood stove, was against the wall to the left, its stovepipe protruding through the side of the building. Near the stove, a crude box overflowed with split wood. Inside walls of the church were simple, white boards, plain and unadorned. The only exception was a picture of Jesus on the wall behind the pulpit. Overhead, a series of wires ran across the building in both directions. Brown burlap curtains hung limply from these wires. The curtains were drawn together during Sunday school to divide the one-room church into classrooms for adults and children. I still remember sitting in Sunday School half listening to Dorothy Cass or Mrs. Caraway teaching the children and half listening to Mrs. Elsie Nitcholas, Mr. Stephenson or my daddy teaching the adults. With no more than a heavy curtain between the classes, total concentration was impossible for a small child.

No notable thing about the building changed from Sunday to Sunday. Steiner Baptist Church was without embellishment, nothing out of the ordinary. It did not matter that the benches were uncomfortable or that the building was cold in the winter and hot in the summer. People came to Steiner Baptist Church for one reason and one reason only. They came to hear God's Word preached.

Steiner Church *sometimes* had lights inside. My dad constructed a delco battery system for the church much like he built for the Steiner store and our home. This system was problematic and extremely temperamental. It chose when to work and when not to work. Looking back, it seems it did not work much of the time. Some Sundays, my dad's time was split between preaching and working on the delco. Maybe God gave him this thorn in the flesh because he fought the call to preach for so long.

When the delco went down, the only lights at the church were kerosene lamps. Thinking about the glow from those lamps as we joined hands at the conclusion of our evening service and sang, "God Be with You Till We Meet Again," brings a rush of feelings to my heart.

During the summer, Steiner Church had a weeklong revival meeting. Men in the church moved the benches, pulpit and piano from the church building to the old brush arbor before the revival started. Songbooks, and paper fans advertising "J.T. Lomax, Funeral Director," were placed on the benches. Each night before the service, someone went to the spring at Steele Creek and filled a jar with cool water for the preacher.

People did not dress up for revival services. Men and boys might wear bib overalls, and hats for the men. Ladies and girls wore plain, cotton dresses. The clothes, though not fancy, were clean. Men pulled their hats off before they went under the arbor. When the piano started playing, children knew to join their parents on the benches. Although the service was under the brush arbor, there was still a feeling of reverence and respect for God's meeting place.

Revivals were special to me. Each night before the service began, the children met to one side of the brush arbor for booster band practice. Probably none of us could carry a tune, but that did not stop us from singing loud and clear. We sang "Jesus Loves Me," "This Little Light of Mine," "Deep and Wide," "A Sunbeam," "Jesus Loves the Little Children," and other songs, complete with all the motions. Sometimes we sang during the revival service. When I stood at the front of the old brush arbor singing with the booster band, I felt sure my voice was better than Shirley Temple's.

While the children had booster band practice, men had prayer meeting. They prayed for lost people in the Steiner area, that God would touch their hardened hearts and they would be saved. As soon as the prayer meeting and booster band practice was over, the revival service started with the congregation singing several old hymns. "The Old Rugged Cross" followed "In the Sweet By and By." At the end of the last hymn before the sermon,

"On Jordan's Stormy Banks I Stand," three or four men walked down the aisle to take the offering. The preacher prayed, and then the men passed baskets to the people on each row of benches. My daddy had given Barbara and me each a nickel before we left home and told us the money was for the offering. He said it was important for us to give money to God because everything we had came from God. I could hardly wait for a basket to reach where I was sitting so I could put my nickel in. The lesson my daddy taught me about tithing has stayed with me all my life.

Then the preaching started. Revival preachers back then did not preach feel-good sermons. Rather, they preached hellfire and brimstone sermons. These sermons made you search your soul to be sure you were right with God. You knew you did not want to go to the place the preacher said you would go if you had never accepted Jesus as your Lord and Savior.

Another thing about revival sermons is they were long. Small children settled down and soon drifted off to sleep on quilts brought from home. Loud "Amen's" all over the brush arbor did not wake the children. The preacher stopped for a drink of the spring water; the water seemed to give him new energy to continue his battle with the devil. Hard, straight-back benches got harder and harder as the sermon went on. Mothers swatted mosquitoes that were buzzing around their sleeping children. Finally invitation time came and the congregation sang several verses of "Lord, I'm Coming Home." People came forward and gave their life to God. Some of these were the ones the men prayed for before the service. Tears of happiness ran down faces. This was what revival was all about.

I thought the last Sunday morning service of the revival would never end. I knew we were going to have dinner on the grounds after church and I could hardly wait. My mother had fried some chickens and made a cake and I was very hungry. When the last prayer ended, the ladies spread dinner on tables under the brush arbor. Everything tasted so good there in the cool shade of the old brush arbor.

After we ate, everyone walked the short distance to Steele Creek for the baptizing. We sang "Shall We Gather at the River," then someone prayed and the baptizing began. As the preacher baptized each new Christian he said, "Buried with Christ in Baptism, Raised to Walk in Newness of Life." When the person came up out of the water, men said "Amen," and "Hallelujah." Sometimes there were tears of happiness once again.

I was not one of those who went forward during the invitation at Steiner Baptist Church; therefore, I was not baptized in Steele Creek. Surely my parents and others prayed that I would accept Jesus, but I did not while we lived at Steiner. We moved to Meridian in mid-October 1949 just after my ninth birthday. During a revival invitation the following summer, God spoke to my heart. I went down the aisle and accepted Jesus as my Lord and Savior. At the conclusion of the revival, Brother McBeth, pastor of Meridian First Baptist Church, baptized me in the church baptistry.

Christmas was a special time at Steiner Church. We had a children's Christmas program on the Sunday night before Christmas. In a small community such as Steiner, this program was the social event of the year. We practiced Christmas carols and speaking parts for weeks before the night of the program. As I go back in time to this distant chapter of my life, the scene at Steiner Baptist Church is vivid in my mind. It is almost as if a reel of film projects images on a giant screen in my head. In my minds-eye, I see angels, shepherds, wise men, Mary and Joseph, all dressed in handmade costumes, on the night of the program. I hear the beginning of the Christmas story read from the book of Luke, "And it came to pass in those days, that there went out a decree from Caesar Augustus that all the world should be taxed."

One year when Brother Worley was our pastor, he brought several members of his family to Steiner Church for the Christmas program. Brother Worley's youngest brother had a part in the program to recite a special Christmas poem. He started strong but soon suffered from stage fright and could not remember the words of the poem. He pulled a piece of paper from his back pocket, unfolded the paper and looked at it for a short while. Then he folded the paper up, put it back into his pocket and continued to recite the poem. Soon he came to another part in the poem that he could not remember. Again, he pulled the paper out, unfolded it and looked at it. After a short while he folded the paper up, put it back into his pocket and said a few more lines of the poem until he again drew a blank. This continued several more times until he finally reached the end of the poem. I can still see him there at the front of the church struggling to remember the words of the poem.

We always had a huge, cedar Christmas tree at the front of the church. This tree reached almost to the top of the ceiling. Various decorations made by the children, along with a few strands of brightly colored lights, hung on the tree. When those lights were turned on, the entire church was transformed into a beautiful wonderland. On the floor at the base of the tree was the most special part of the evening—the gift each child would receive at the conclusion of the program.

The children gathered at the front of the church at the end of the evening. Suddenly the back door opened and Santa came bursting into the church. Oh, the excitement on the children's faces as Santa called their names and beckoned them to come to the Christmas tree. One by one, each child received a small cellophane bag containing an orange, an apple, some nuts and a few pieces of ribbon candy. It is impossible to put into words how special this gift was to a child growing up in Steiner, Texas, in the 1940's.

The Meridian Years...

Lake Whitney—The End of an Era
Meridian—A New Beginning

The Brazos River begins in eastern New Mexico and flows generally southeast across Texas to the Gulf of Mexico. When early settlements began to develop along the Brazos, the river often got out of banks and flooded some areas. In the 1930's, the Brazos River Authority decided to build thirteen reservoirs at various locations on the Brazos all the way to the Gulf of Mexico.

The Works Progress Administration, or WPA, a New Deal Depression Recovery Agency, built Morris Sheppard Dam situated primarily in Palo Pinto County. This dam, named after a Senator from Texas, was completed in 1941. Water conservation and flood control were the main functions of the dam; however, two generators were installed to supply limited power for the area. Morris Sheppard Dam created Possum Kingdom Lake, the first reservoir built on the Brazos River.

Lake Whitney, in Bosque and Hill Counties, was the second reservoir built on the Brazos River. Plans developed for the Whitney Dam in the early 1940's. The dam would create the Lake Whitney reservoir, improve flood control and generate power for the surrounding area. Authorization for Whitney Dam came in 1944 and the project began in earnest in 1946.

The construction of Whitney Dam provided job opportunities in the immediate area. Kopperl School reaped the benefits of these job opportunities as families moved into the area because of those jobs. One of the new students at Kopperl School, Mike McNeill, became good friends with my cousin, Janet Cole. Through the years, this friendship continued until Janet's death on August 25, 2008. Mike married one of my good friends, Judy Holt, Doctor Holt's daughter from Meridian.

After several years of construction, Whitney Dam was completed in 1951 and the power plant began operation in 1953. The Army Corps of

Engineers maintains the dam built directly on the county line dividing Hill and Bosque Counties.

Soon public concern began to surface over the proposal to build thirteen flood-control dams on the Brazos. During the fall of 1958, John Graves made a canoe trip down a stretch of the Brazos River between Possum Kingdom Lake and Lake Whitney. Mr. Graves wrote a book, *Goodbye to a River*, about his canoe trip. In the book, he described himself as "a concerned citizen" who had a fear of the "drowning" effect thirteen dams would have on the Brazos River. The success of this book was a major influence on the decision to not build all thirteen dams. DeCordova Bend Dam in Hood County was the third and last dam built on the Brazos River. Lake Granbury reservoir is the result of the DeCordova Bend Dam completed in 1969.

Before the Whitney Dam and Lake Whitney reservoir project began, Steiner citizens knew the Steiner area would be in the flood plain of Lake Whitney. Although the building project began in 1946, two years passed before serious deliberations seemed necessary for the Cole family. Finally my parents began to make plans for moving our family from Steiner.

Though I did not fully understand the significance of moving, one chapter of my life was quickly ending and another chapter about to begin. Soon the simple life as I knew it in Steiner, Texas would no longer exist. As I stood on the threshold of this new horizon, I was totally unaware of the changes ahead of me. The family living quarters behind Steiner store was the only home I had ever known. The old kitchen served up my meals and was where I played on top of the icehouse. My bare feet ran carefree over the dusty grounds surrounding the Steiner Store. The whistle of the train as it passed through Steiner was a familiar, comforting sound that I had grown accustomed to over the brief nine years of my lifetime. Inside the store the long, glass candy case was my daily companion. Neighbors gathering to make a freezer of ice cream, trips to the Wallace place to pick cotton and eat sardines and pork and beans in the shade of the wagon, swimming in Steele Creek, watching the stars at night as we slept outside in the summertime, revival services under the old brush arbor, corralling stick horses and eating green grape pies with my friend, Sherry Brown, would no longer be part of my life. Soon there would be no more games of croquet or horseshoes, no more feeling the squish of sand between my toes on the croquet court.

The year 1949 was well advanced as I celebrated my ninth birthday on September 15. My fourth grade year at Kopperl School was in full swing under the tutelage of Miss Joyce Andrews. I loved school and fourth grade was going much better for me than third grade. My sister, Barbara, was in Miss Phinney's fifth grade class just down the hall from me.

My dad's brother, Uncle Lois Cole, drove the Kopperl school bus that picked Barbara and me up at Steiner store each morning. When the bus stopped at the Steiner store, Brown, Herring, McCurdy, Wood, Webb, Townley, Rich, Brooks, Duke, Pinnell, Williams and Payne children, to name a few, were already on the bus. After leaving Steiner store, the bus crossed the railroad tracks and stopped to pick up Sherry Brown. Sherry still lived where Maxine and Pauline Payne used to live, next door to Ma and Pa Cole. From there, the bus picked up Charles Steen, La Vere and Darrell Vinson, Gerald Hadley and others who lived near the Steiner store. After several more miles, the bus crossed Steele Creek and stopped to pick up Robert Bachhofer, Mearl and Pearl Etchison and others before arriving at Kopperl School.

My sister, Bonnie, was no longer in school, as she graduated from Kopperl High School in May 1948. Following her graduation, she worked for the "Triple A" office in Meridian alongside Ruth Seidel, Margaret Ryan (later Margaret Woolley) and Loretta Brown, Sherry's mother. After working there for a while, Bonnie went to work for Omar Robinson at the Bosque County Tax Assessor-Collector's Office. Elva Seidel was the Chief Deputy Tax Collector. Bonnie worked for Mr. Robinson until she married Norvil Flatt in May 1954. Interestingly, I too worked at the Bosque County Tax Office when I finished high school. The Tax Collector at that time was Earl Behringer. Elva was still the Chief Deputy Tax Collector when I worked there. Following Mr. Behringer's stint, Elva successfully ran for Bosque County Tax Assessor-Collector, an honor that was long overdue.

Once my parents made the decision to move to Meridian all wheels started in motion. The land owned by my parents, two hundred fifty acres known as the "Wallace Place" and one hundred fifteen additional acres that joined the Wallace place, was "taken" by the United States of America in late 1949. The government paid my parents forty dollars an acre for this land. Some of the acreage was later determined to not be in the flood plain and my parents bought this land back. They sold the land to J.F. "Pop" Sample and his wife, Vivian, in 1954. Mr. And Mrs. Sample built "Pop Sample's Development" on this land located on the shores of Lake Whitney. All of the land in the lower part of the Wallace place is under water now and has been since the completion of Lake Whitney Dam.

My parents used part of the money from the sale of their Steiner land to purchase a three-bedroom home in Meridian from Felix Shafer. They bought the house on August 30, 1949 and we moved to Meridian in October of that same year. Our new home was situated on Main Street and would be where Bonnie, Barbara and I lived until we married. My brother, Mearl, continues to live in this house.

I will never forget the first time I saw my new home. To me, the house was like a fairy tale come true. The house and detached garage had a fresh coat of white paint. A sidewalk led to the front porch of the house and divided the well-groomed yard. A trimmed hedge separated our house from the house next door.

Inside the house, the living room, dining room and three bedrooms had beautiful hardwood floors. Every room in the house had long windows with window screens on the outside. This was quite different, as my Steiner home had few windows and no window screens. Our home in Meridian did not have air-conditioning, but few homes in the early 1950's did. We left the windows open to help cool the house.

As you entered each room of my new home, there was a light switch by the door. Certainly a simple light switch is nothing out of the ordinary in today's world; however, it was some phenomena to my sister, Barbara, and me. Since our Steiner home did not have light switches, we almost wore the switch in our shared bedroom out before the new wore off.

Another thing Barbara and I marveled at was the telephone. We had a crank-type telephone in the Steiner store; however, we could not call anyone locally because our telephone was the only one in Steiner. In Meridian, we had a dial telephone and could call locally with very few turns of the dial. For example, if we wanted to call the Capitol Theater to find out what movie was showing, we dialed "21." If we wanted to call the Holt-Archer Clinic to make an appointment, we dialed "30." Making a telephone call in those days was much easier than today.

We did not have a television for several years after we moved to Meridian, but few people in Meridian had televisions in the early 1950's. It was simple to know who had a television and who did not. You just had to look for the big, tall antenna on the rooftop. One of the first in Meridian to have a television was Superintendent Perry and his family. Margie Belle used to come to school and tell us what shows she had watched the night before. From what I saw on the early televisions, there was more "snow" than pictures on the screen.

The most extraordinary room in our new home was the bathroom. There was a bathtub with hot and cold running water. Finally the number-three bathtub could be retired. As wonderful as the bathtub was, the most spectacular thing was we no longer had to go outside and visit the outhouse. Who would have imagined having an entire room dedicated to meeting their personal needs?

My entire family was pleased with our new home in Meridian; however, my mother was especially overjoyed when she met some neighbors living diagonally across the street from us. According to my mother, Mero and Katie Lee Hegar, had a "cement storm cellar" and had invited her to join them in the cellar anytime a storm came up. My mother accepted the invitation and went to their cellar many times during the years.

My dad was not impressed at all when he heard about the Hegar's cellar. In fact, he commented, "Yes, I figure a storm will be the death of Ray. She will probably get hit by a car crossing the street going to the Hegar's cellar!"

There is a bit of irony regarding Meridian being chosen as my family's new home. My old home, Steiner, was named after Doctor Josephus M. Steiner, a soldier and post physician at Fort Graham, near Steiner. In 1854 the town of Meridian began on twenty acres donated by Andrew Montgomery and one hundred acres donated by the same Doctor Josephus M. Steiner that the community of Steiner was named after.

Barbara and I finished the first six-weeks of school in Kopperl and enrolled in school in Meridian for the second six-weeks. My new fourth grade teacher was Mrs. Eddie Parks Martin. Barbara's fifth grade teacher was Mrs. Robert Wells. Curtis Evans was the Grammar School Principal and W.C. Perry was Superintendent of Schools. Mr. Perry's daughter, Margie Belle, was in my grade.

I loved going to school in Meridian just as much as I did in Kopperl. My Meridian school days were not as long because I did not have to ride the bus in the mornings and afternoons. The Meridian school was a new adventure for me. If I close my eyes really tight and listen carefully, I can hear the shrill ringing of the school bell as it signaled the start of a new school day. The rustle of Mrs. Burch's freshly starched school-nurse uniform, and the plopping sounds made by Lee Erickson cleaning the halls with his big rag mop echo in my ears. I can picture Mrs. Gillaspie, Mrs. Hunter, Mrs. Farmer, Mrs. Martin, Mrs. Wells, Mrs. Richards or Mr. Strother ushering their students into the classrooms. The aroma from the hot rolls and peanut butter cookies that Mrs. Greenwade served in the school cafeteria permeates my nostrils. And I will never forget how the duplicating fluid smelled on the sheets of paper with the purple writing.

Infantile paralysis, or Polio, was running rampant during my elementary school days. I knew firsthand the devastating effects of polio as my cousin, Janet Cole, contracted this disease. One school day our teacher sent notes home with us instructing our parents to bring us to the school cafeteria that evening for an important meeting regarding polio. When we got to the cafeteria, medical personnel handed out pamphlets with information about the illness. Nurses dropped a few drops of liquid polio vaccine onto sugar cubes and all of the children walked by and received a vaccine-laced sugar cube.

As in any small community, tragedy struck Meridian without warning. I was in the fifth grade and Gloria Nickels was a pretty little girl in the fourth grade. Gloria's peers liked her due to her friendliness and bright smile. One day Gloria attended school as usual. After school, Gloria was at home playing when an accidental shooting ended her short life. Gloria's burial site is near my grandparents' graves in the Meridian Cemetery. I often walk over and look at her tombstone. Gloria's fourth grade school picture smiles back at me from her tombstone, her dark hair curled into ringlets.

Soon after we got settled in Meridian, my dad bought several lots on highway 174 toward Morgan. He and my brother, Mearl, built a service station, grocery store and automotive garage on these lots. My dad and brother operated this business for over twenty years until my dad's health failed. At that time, my dad sold the service station to Joe Allen. This location is where Joe now has his wrecking yard business.

In April 1950, my dad purchased four hundred seventy-five acres of land from S.S. Nichols. This land was located just off highway six toward Iredell. There was a house on the land and the Lee McCurdy family moved from Steiner into this house.

After my dad bought the land from Mr. Nichols, he purchased cows and continued ranching on this land much like he had done on the Wallace place at Steiner. One day my dad went to the weekly auction sale to buy some cows but bought goats instead. I overheard my parents talking about his purchase and my mother asked him why he bought goats rather than cows. My dad told her he bought the goats because he thought they were sheep. I remember thinking it probably was not a good idea for my dad to be a rancher if he did not know the difference between goats and sheep. Later I found out my dad actually said he bought the goats because he thought they were "cheap," not "sheep".

Following our move to Meridian, my dad preached at the new location of Steiner Baptist Church on Sunday afternoons. Our family attended Meridian First Baptist Church on Sunday mornings, Sunday evenings and Wednesday evenings, and Steiner Baptist Church on Sunday afternoons. My dad also preached many funerals at different churches or at Brister-Lawson Funeral Home.

Barbara and I were active in Sunday school, church services and choir at our new Meridian Church. We also attended Vacation Bible School each summer. In the past, Steiner Baptist Church occasionally offered Vacation Bible School in the summer. Recently, I was looking through an old scrapbook and discovered a Steiner VBS certificate awarded to me on August 13, 1948. The following names were on the certificate: A.T. Worley, Pastor, Odell Steen, Sunday School Superintendent, Shirley Payne, VBS Director and Bonnie Cole, Teacher.

After living in Steiner for the first nine years of my life, the town of Meridian truly amazed me. I was like a kid at Christmas with all the different things to amuse me. There was the Capitol Movie Theater in town, a drive-in theater at the circle, and a second drive-in on the Clifton highway near where Rex and Ruth Ann Anderson now live. I spent many Saturday afternoons with my girlfriends at the Capitol Theater watching western movies. When the new Three-D movies came out, we were there with our special paper glasses cheering on the heroes. After a few years, the movies were not the main reason we went to the Capitol Theater. Several girls around my age began to notice a group of boys from Cranfills Gap who came to the movies. Jake and Cecil Wimberly, Marc Johnson, Darryl Olson, James Johnson and others from Cranfills Gap caught our eyes. We became friends with these boys and wrote letters back and forth during the week. Two girls in my grade went on to marry two of these boys. My cousin, Betty Ann Knudson, married Marc Johnson. Joann Gann married Jake Wimberly. Both couples are still married today.

Movies were cheap in the early 1950's. A quarter bought a movie ticket for nine cents with enough for popcorn and a coke and money left over. After the movie, I often walked to Sheppard's Drug Store for a dip of ice cream. I can still see Joe Sheppard taking the ice cream scoop out of the container of water, shaking it off and scooping that five-cent dip of vanilla, strawberry or chocolate ice cream. He turned the scoop round and round in the cylinder container of ice cream until he was sufficiently pleased the scoop was full and running over. Then he served the ice cream up in a cold, glass dish with a small metal spoon. Now let me tell you, Blue Bell never tasted so good.

The skating rink at the circle was a favorite hangout for kids in Meridian. As often as possible, I went to the rink and skated round and round on the old oak floor for a couple of hours. I was always hungry after all that exercise, so I would go next door to Lowry's Drive-in and get a fifteen-cent hamburger and nickel coke. The skating rink was in the building now occupied by Rare Motor Sports. Lowry's Drive-in was where Pappa Docs now is.

In the summer, there were additional things to do. Our neighborhood had many kids near my age that I played with. Mickey and Leland Stewart, Sue and Nell Sheppard, Sara Lynn and Ruth Ann Wreay, Conrad and Jim Tom Archer, Larry Sam Lawson, Lou Jean Johnston and Brenda Rickard all lived within rock-throwing distance of my home. There was someone to play with anytime I went outside. Unlike Steiner, there were sidewalks in front of our houses. We rode our bicycles up and down these sidewalks or skated on our four-wheeled metal skates with the skate key on a string around our neck. We gathered in someone's backyard, built tents and forts and had imaginary battles for hours at a time. A game of football or softball sometimes lasted until dark. We got together and traded funny books or baseball cards and played long games of Monopoly. Our parents never worried about where we were or what we were doing because most mothers did not work outside the home in the early 1950's. No matter whose children were playing at a friend's house, the mother felt free to discipline those children along with their own children, or at the very least, send them home.

I loved playing at Conrad and Jim Tom Archer's house. Their dad was Doctor Archer, and they were the first people I knew who had a maid to cook their meals and keep the house clean. Even though the maid did most of the cooking, Mrs. Archer liked to make cookies. Her specialty was peanut butter cookies and she shared these delicious cookies with all the neighborhood kids. It was interesting to watch Mrs. Archer make these cookies. First, she tore off a long piece of waxed paper to cover her work surface. Then she mixed the cookies in a large bowl that was sitting in the middle of the waxed paper. When she finished making the cookies, she put the dirty dishes in the sink, rolled up the paper and threw it in the trash. I was amazed at how clean the drain board was after she had the cookies made.

Sara Lynn and Ruth Ann Wreay lived next door to the Archer's. One hot, summer afternoon,

Barbara and I were playing at the Wreay's house with several other children. Since their house was directly across the road from our house, we noticed a car pulling into our driveway. We soon identified the visitors as a former pastor and his family. This particular preacher did not believe girls and ladies should wear shorts. Barbara and I had a BIG problem—we both had on shorts, and we knew we could not go home with shorts on. We really did not know what to do because we figured the preacher's family would spend the night at our house. Finally our mother gathered some long pants and sent Mearl across the street without the visitors knowing what was going on. We quickly changed clothes and went home to visit with our company.

Whereas Steiner offered swimming in Steele Creek or the Brazos River, Meridian was totally modernized with a swimming pool complete with diving boards and a lifeguard. Dorann Gill and I spent many summer afternoons at the swimming pool with all the other kids. Dorann was a very good swimmer and an exceptionally good diver. I was, and still am, afraid of water that is deeper than I am tall. While Dorann wowed everyone with her swimming and diving expertise, I impressed no one as I splashed around in the shallow end of the pool.

After Dorann and I swam for several hours, we sometimes spent the night together at one of our houses. I remember once I spent the night with Dorann and we went to a party at her church, the Methodist Church. This was the old Methodist Church on Morgan Street that had the big basement underneath the church sanctuary. This basement was a really neat place for parties. When I was in Junior High the Methodist young people had dances in this basement. Of course my strict Baptist parents did not allow me to go to these "Methodist" dances.

A small circus or carnival occasionally came to town. Kids from all over Meridian and the surrounding area waited anxiously for the tent to be set up and tickets to go on sale. One year a different kind of traveling show made an appearance in Meridian. Unlike a circus or carnival, this was a play. The show company provided the script and costumes and local folks were the actors. Weeks before the show arrived, posters all around town announced an audition for parts in the show. Finally my opportunity had arrived. I felt sure since my name was almost Shirley Temple Cole, this was my chance to kick off my acting career. I did get a part in the play, but it was a very small part with no more than two or three lines. The play was on the school stage and the main thing I remember about the show is Grady and Elizabeth Wreay's act. They sang and danced to the music, "Too Old to Cut the Mustard Anymore." Their performance just about brought the house down.

Soon after we moved to Meridian, my dad visited the Snow Buick and J.T. Lomax Chrysler-Plymouth dealerships and came home driving a brand new Plymouth. My mother asked my dad where in the world he got the money to buy a new car. My dad told her Tucker Glenn gave him the money. I did not know much about Tucker Glenn, other than he ran the Farmers State Bank in Meridian, but I thought it was very nice of him to give my dad money to buy a new car.

I felt we had arrived—that we were truly "up town" now that we lived in a place like Meridian and had a new car to boot. It was really something to ride up and down paved roads in our new car and see all that Meridian had to offer. Downtown Meridian was anchored by the courthouse square with businesses across the street from the courthouse on all four sides. Certainly, my early impression of Meridian was influenced by my life at Steiner. Compared to Steiner, Meridian was a major metropolis.

When we moved to Meridian, my beloved grandparents, Ma and Pa Cole moved there also. Their new home was just a few houses up the street from our home, and they continued to be an important part of my life.

In November 1949 my best friend, Sherry Brown, moved from Steiner to Morgan. We continued to be friends, but our friendship was put on hold until we both entered high school. At that time, Sherry drove eight miles each school day from Morgan to Meridian to attend high school. We were once again inseparable and shared so much during our high school years. One other Steiner friend, Kenneth Herring, had moved from Steiner to Meridian with his family. Kenneth, Sherry and I were all in the same grade and graduated from Meridian High School together in 1958.

In the beginning, I told you this story was about a little girl who grew up to be an ordinary person with an ordinary story to tell. I have pretty much told this story, but in the process, I have changed my mind. This is not just an ordinary story. It is a story about my life at Steiner from the time I was born until I was nine years old, as well as a few years of my life in Meridian. No one else could tell this story because no one else walked in my shoes.

Writing my story down on paper has been easy at times and difficult at other times; however, I have enjoyed the trip down memory lane so very much.

Reflections...

As an adult, I have gone back to Steiner many times. I have walked the grounds of the old Steiner store building and surrounding outbuildings. Was it just my imagination, or did I hear echoes of laughter from the many good times I had living at Steiner?

There are no buildings, no croquet court, nothing remaining from the past with the exception of the storm cellar. Standing in front of the old, caved in cellar brought a flood of emotions to my mind. Thinking about my mother pulling on that rope on the inside of the cellar while my daddy tried his best to get the door open from the outside reminded me of just how fortunate I am to have so many happy memories of my childhood years at Steiner.

I am totally amazed when I look back on those years. When my parents got married in December

1929, they, like others of their generation, had nothing. Following their marriage they spent their time and energy surviving the depression years. They worked hard and lived conservatively to provide the necessities for their family. Surely they did not make much money operating the Steiner store, blacksmith shop, gristmill, feed store and automobile garage. Yet somehow they managed to save enough money to buy three hundred and sixty-five acres of land in the Steiner area. The only possible explanation I can think of is that God was very good to my family.

When I recall my early life at Steiner, I realize those nine years were much different from the world I live in today. Though I did not have television or other modern conveniences, I do not feel I was deprived in any way. Times were hard, life was simple, but pleasures far outnumbered the bad times. My childhood years spent at Steiner were wonderful years that I feel so blessed to have had. I think about those years often and know how lucky I was to have grown up in Steiner, Texas, a place that laid the foundation for the remainder of my life. I realize that the Steiner community and the people living there may have been poor on the surface, but in the most important ways, they were not poor at all. Though I did not comprehend it as a child, I feel I was remarkably privileged to have passed through Steiner at the time that I did. Those years are stamped indelibly on my memory as the most significant years of my life!

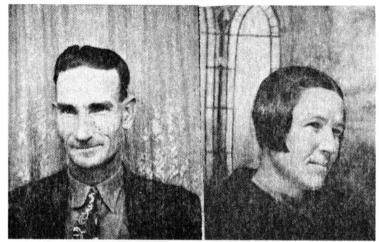

My parents, Evins and Ray Cole-1935

**Cole Family members. Steiner store in the background.
Shirley in mother's arms in front row-1941**

**Front Row L-R: Barbara and Shirley Cole.
Back Row L-R: Bonnie and Mearl Cole.
Kitchen door in background-1941**

Barbara and Shirley Cole(with bottle)-1941

**L-R: Gloria Shafer(holding Shirley), Bonnie, Mearl and
Barbara Cole, and Maurice Shafer-1941**

My Grandparents, J.W. and Leola Cole(Ma and Pa), with Shirley in front. Train Depot in background.-1942

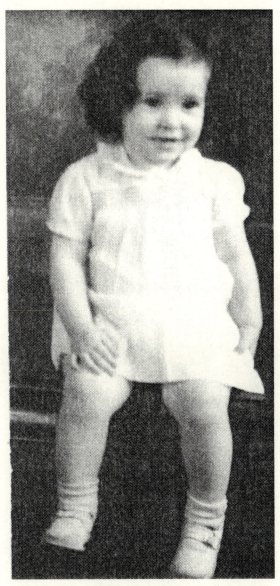

Shirley Cole-1942

L-R: Joe Warren Cass, Shirley and Barbara Cole. Blacksmith shop and daddy's automotive garage in background.-1942

**My Dad, Evins Cole, holding(L-R) Barbara
and Shirley Cole-1943**

Evins, Ray, and Shirley Cole.
Steiner store and flying red horse
(Magnolia) gas pump in background-1946

L-R: Barbara Cole, Sherry Brown, and Shirley Cole-1947

Front L-R: Shirley and Barbara Cole
Back L-R: Bonnie and Mearl Cole-1948

Laura Wallace in front of her house

Shirley Cole after being promoted to third grade, midterm, 1949

Steiner Baptist Church - This picture was taken after building moved to Poeville area on Buddy Nitcholas' land in 1950. This is the same building built in 1908